MW00887473

From Monsters to Miracles

Parent-Driven Recovery Tools that Work

Written by

Anette Edens, PhD

With the generous support and funding of

The Fondren Foundation
&
Cornerstone Recovery, Inc.

ISBN: 978-1-4834-46806 (sc)
ISBN: 978-1-4834-4682-0 (hc)
ISBN: 978-1-4834-4681-3 (e)

Library of Congress Control Number: 2016902465

Lulu Publishing Services rev. date: 3/29/2016

Contents

Foreword

Dr. Anette Edens has led Cornerstone Recovery (www.cornerstonerecovery.org) for nearly two decades and now provides a guidebook for parents dealing with their child's addiction. Anette is a parent herself and has worked with many hundreds of parents and their kids. Parents *can* be the "antidrug" but need help understanding the insidious nature of addiction and how powerful recovery can be in preventing the destruction of the home. Parent participation in recovery is key, *indeed virtually essential*, to long-term success. This well-written and informative book provides a toolbox for families where addiction has thrown the family into chaos. It could be titled *Addiction—A Family Disease.*

Family system is truly a literal term; the family is an interdependent system, like a mobile. When all parts (mom, dad, kids) are in balance, the system functions well. But if you unbalance one part (addicted child), the system becomes imbalanced, and all the parts are out of place. Relationships are broken—trust is gone. And shame prevents us from seeking the very solution that will help us—others in the same boat.

Let me emphasize what is a common misunderstanding; alcohol and drugs are not truly the problem, although they seem to be. Rather, they are the quick-fix solution used to cope with and medicate the pain and fear felt inside by the addicted, entitled child who feels like his world is falling apart. Addiction is an "outside solution for an inside job." It's a "dis-ease." As Dr. Edens points out, "Entitlement sucks out any self-esteem they may have developed. It is a parasite that overwhelms its victim, tricking him or her into thinking he or she is owed." When reality strikes and addicts realize they are not the "center of the universe," fear becomes overwhelming, and they seek relief in drugs and high-risk behavior (see "Becoming Mature," in Chapter 5). This book supports parents in raising children whose insides match their outsides, who are resilient to the speed bumps that life presents, and who do not feel entitled.

So, if you even suspect your child is using drugs or alcohol or engaging in any other destructive behavior, put away that cute baby picture image of your little "darling," and read this book. Become willing to seek help and join the thousands of families who enjoy recovery.

Scott F. Basinger, PhD

Acknowledgments

This book was inspired and encouraged by Leland Fondren, who recognized the need for a concise manual for parents facing their adolescent's substance abuse and addiction. Without his encouragement, this work would have remained a bucket-list item on hold for my retirement. I greatly appreciate his help and support and the generosity of the Fondren Foundation, who believed in the value of such a book and funded this project.

The manuscript is based upon a series of workshops that I developed from my experience and research with parents over the past twenty years. The workshops were funded by the Fondren Foundation and offered to parents over a two-year period, allowing me the opportunity to organize my thoughts. I was extremely fortunate to have been able to host my workshops in The Hope and Healing Center and Institute at St. Martin's Church of Houston. Their facilities and staff are warm and lovely, and I am humbled by their support of this work.

Cornerstone Recovery's incredibly talented staff has been supportive and patient as I closed my door to them for hours at a time. My board of directors has been tireless, encouraging, challenging, and brilliant. I am grateful for each of them and for the opportunity to work at this incredible organization.

Dr. Scott Basinger, who wrote the foreword to this book, is a brilliant academician, a master of recovery and intervention, and has become a dear friend. I am thrilled that he has had the interest and taken his time to review this manuscript. I also want to thank Tammie Gross,

Cindy Roop, and Brittany Fondren who read, corrected, and critiqued this book. My dear friend, Dr. Patricia Mahlstedt, put her whole heart into reading, providing feedback, and offering editorial suggestions for which I am incredibly grateful. I am truly blessed to have such smart and loving women in my life.

To Jocelyn, who playfully insisted on singing every single verse of "American Pie" around the campfire, while a reluctant group of wounded moms slowly remembered how to laugh. Her joy was infectious.

Jocelyn McNulty
1956–2012

Chapter 1

WE BEGIN WHERE WE ARE

....

You change for two reasons:
Either you learn enough that you want to, or
you've been hurt enough that you have to.
—Unknown

....

I never met a parent of a troubled teen who wasn't trying to figure out what went wrong. We thought we were in control—that we knew what we were doing. We raise our children pretty much by what feels like instinct, based upon what we learned as a child, by experiencing what our parents did or what we wish they had done. But when our child begins to veer off course our "instincts" can undermine our effectiveness. We are perplexed. We try so hard, love our kids so much, and they withdraw further and further into their world of dark secrets while we watch with agonizing powerlessness. We feel lost. I wish we could skip that piece of the process, but it is part of the journey for many of us.

I have seen many families who had practically lost all hope, some with problems that I have experienced firsthand. I did not always negotiate my parenting challenges well. I have learned from my failures, each of which presented an opportunity for me to either grow or to wallow in pain. I have revisited them through my work over the past twenty years with parents and their adolescents whose substance abuse and addictions, eating disorders, mental illnesses, and traumas have brought them to seek help. This book is my effort to share my experience, strength, and hope as a mother and as a professional who has worked with hundreds of families whose children have become addicted to drugs.

This book is about parenting intentionally, adjusting and adapting to changes in our culture and to the developmental, biological, and social challenges that our children face as they mature. We are not prepared to effectively adapt to adolescents' needs—particularly adolescents who are in trouble in a culture we don't quite understand and with brains that are not yet capable of making healthy choices.

The stories that families bring to my office are heartbreaking. Teens have no idea what their parents are going through, and parents have very limited knowledge of their teen's experiences. Adolescents hide their lives from their parents and are blatantly dishonest when using any mind-altering chemical. Further, our objectivity regarding our own child is flawed. We therefore fail to see what is right in front of us and rarely know that our child's drug and/or alcohol use is out of control until they are deeply involved.

Expectations & Defenses

We do not want to believe that our child will break the rules. Some of us don't have explicit rules, but instead deal with problems as they arise. We tell them that mind-altering chemicals are bad for them. Even with clearly articulated rules, many of us don't expect the rules to be violated. We expect that the rule itself will be enough to deter any wrong choices.

Teens break rules and lie. Those of us who are not ready to recognize when our child is lying to our faces lose our ability to see the child and reality as it is. Our defense mechanisms emerge. We rationalize, deny, project.

We buy into our child's masterfully crafted scenarios justifying their inappropriate behavior, convincing ourselves they are reasonable. Here are some examples that I have heard:

- It isn't as bad as it seems.
- This is very common among this age group—thus normal.
- The drugs in my child's pocket belong to friend whose parents are insane.
- This is just a phase and will end soon.
- I smoked some marijuana in my youth and I would feel like a hypocrite if I complained about his doing the same thing.
- He has only been *experimenting* with heroin.

This is the child who we have nurtured through life, with whom we have built a mutually trusting relationship. We try to hold on to that trust. Ultimately we watch in disbelief as our troubled child plays with our heart in callous disregard for the pain he inflicts, ignorant of his own fragile mortality. Not knowing what to do, many of us just do more for them and protect them more fiercely, believing that we will eventually awaken from this incredibly painful nightmare.

Eventually, with enough repeated experience, we begin to see clearly. It isn't just going away as we had hoped. We scramble to fix things. We try to control our teen. We might try to scare some sense into them.

We talk to them, threaten them, and ground them, but this just alienates them further and nothing changes. We stalk them. We use tracking devices in their phones or cars and surveillance systems in their rooms. We monitor the keystrokes on their computers and texts on their phones. We look for hard evidence in order to justify a confrontation, believing that once we confront them with direct evidence they will come clean, feel remorse, and this moment of truth will change everything. It doesn't.

Why Questions

When our early efforts are futile, we start searching for other clues to illuminate this dark place. Why would our children take this dangerous, self-destructive path? *Why* questions are a waste of time. If pressed, we can hypothesize and theorize about why people have taken the paths they have taken, but in this moment what matters most is that we recognize our power to adjust the path.

There are countless stories. Each child is different. Each family's story is different.

As parents, we feel that answering the *Why* question will lead us to the solution. What really happens is that we get mired in a futile quest for the origins of the problems our family is facing. While spinning our wheels in the muck of the past, our energy is wasted and we are exhausted.

This search for the *Why* of our predicament is usually driven by a secret hope to absolve ourselves of blame for this nightmare. We need answers, but this is the wrong question.

Shame & Blame

So, if not *Why,* then maybe the question is, *How did this happen?*

When we have a disease and the organ that is diseased is our brain, our behavior gets odd, and people get uncomfortable. People talk. When the disease is addiction, people judge the disease as a character flaw. Those afflicted with alcoholism or addiction are judged harshly, as are their families. We may have even felt this way ourselves. We judge our children and we judge ourselves.

We are filled with shame. We may try to keep our child's problem a secret, although the misery of it consumes us. We live in a culture that is hard on parents, and the stigma of substance abuse and addiction is powerful. *How can my child be doing this to me?* It feels personal. It isn't about us.

Our shame can turn into anger. It is easy to blame the other parent or those "bad" friends, the school, the culture, etc. This tactic is all about our egos trying to relieve our shame. It makes both us and our children victims and powerless and is a waste of precious time. We cannot solve the problem by blaming ourselves or others and hoping that everyone else will change.

Substance abuse is not a moral failure. Addiction is a chronic and treatable medical condition (Barry, McGinty, et al., 2014). Addiction is relatively more treatable, with much fewer long-term difficulties than other serious mental illnesses, but the stigma horrifies parents.

Pain Motivates a New Beginning

The harsh reality of our family's misery and our inability to fix it is devastatingly painful. When we finally seek professional help with our troubled adolescents, our hopes have been shattered. I can identify with this. Often living in terror that our child will die, we are bewildered that the person who now lives with us bears no resemblance to the child we once knew. We are lost in our powerlessness yet continue to hold on to the illusion that if we try hard enough we can control our child's behavior. We cannot, and although terrified, depressed, angry, and ashamed, we try harder.

At some point, we realize that we need outside, experienced help. Even though this moment is the culmination of a long series of events, in this moment we recognize that we are completely powerless to control our child's spiral toward self-destruction. It is painful and bewildering. We become open to new ideas, new ways to relate to our children, and new ways to think about parenting.

Emotional pain compels us to seek relief. The process of becoming motivated to change is the same for the parent as it is for the addicted teen. Things have to become painful, and our powerlessness has to hit us hard.

We may not always look for relief in the right places, but the pain will continue until we find what we need to do in order to become part of the solution. We begin to let go of appearances and talk to friends, professionals, and organizations. We read books. We pray. We look outside of our own knowledge to find a solution for what feels like the child's problem. The average family spends three years sending their child to various kinds of professionals before engaging in parent-driven recovery (Cates & Cummings, 2003).

Parents who show up at my office are likely to have watched in horror as their precious child devolved into a dark and miserable creature, unrecognizable in his cold disregard for all who love him. They have spent countless dollars on therapies that have been ineffective. They have paid for hospitalizations and residential treatments that are almost immediately followed by relapse (Sannibale et al., 2003). Parents enter the recovery world hopeless, defeated, financially drained, afraid for their child's life, ashamed, and broken. Their marriages have become fragile, are disintegrating, or are already shattered from the trauma.

We begin where we are, in this moment, and quit obsessing about the past. We begin today with solutions.

Letting Go Is Not Giving Up

When we aren't satisfied with where our life is taking us, we have the ability to adjust whatever we are doing that is leading us along this path. If life isn't working out so well, most of us try to change everything and everyone around us, which sets us up for failure and alienates everyone we are trying to control.

Change isn't so easy. It's particularly hard to change when we are firmly entrenched in the position that we are right and everyone else is wrong. From this perspective there is no room for improvement. Yet our best thinking and our best efforts have delivered us exactly to the place that we stand today. If we want something to change, we must courageously accept the challenge, surrender our egos, and humbly adjust our own behavior.

This humility lets us give up the illusion of our superior wisdom. There is hope to be found in the experiences of those who have already been where we are. We can now choose to approach problems with curiosity and willingness, to allow ourselves to become teachable, to keep learning. My children have provided those opportunities for me, moments in which in spite of my training and experience, I had to humbly become open to the wisdom, observations, and suggestions of others.

We can only change ourselves. We cannot change or fix our child. However, when we make personal changes that create the environment in which our child can choose a new path, we recover our power as parents and become an essential part of the solution. This is why we need to learn and change.

The Metaphor of the Soil

The metaphor of the soil and the diseased plant is often used in recovery circles. We can remove the struggling plant from its soil and nurture it to health in a greenhouse, but by returning it to the soil of its origin—depleted of nutrients, dry, and dark—we virtually guarantee the ultimate relapse of the plant to its diseased state.

We are the soil, and we have to change in order to nurture the health of our troubled children. For this reason, recovery needs to be a family journey. In my experience, *parental engagement in the recovery process is the single most powerful predictor of the adolescent's long-term recovery.*

We Need *The Village?*

Our closest friends, although comfortable, cannot really help us move forward unless they have been where we are. We need people who can offer experience as the parent of a troubled or addicted teen. We need the support of people who can love and accept us, empathize with our struggles, hold us accountable to healthy actions, and never judge or criticize us. We need to see the successes and genuine intimacy in the families who have preceded us in healing. This kind of support can be found among those parents who have been through the nightmare and are living with solutions. Most of us feel immediate relief when we meet other people who have been through what we are going through, particularly when they have experienced relief from this pain.

There are recovery support groups in most communities for family members of addicts and alcoholics. Increasingly there are such recovery support groups strictly for parents. We do not need to carry the burden alone.

There is much to learn. Our best thinking is exhausted and we need new ideas and strategies. This book offers *parent-driven recovery* concepts, and will be most helpful if used in concert with participation in a strong recovery support group.

Often parents tell me that although they began their involvement in the recovery world to support their child, they remain involved for themselves. The simplicity and serenity of a life lived in recovery are compelling. The personal growth, using the simple parent-driven recovery principles taught herein, are life-changing.

Most of us live on autopilot, unaware of the choices that are available to us if we just quit thinking we know something and instead get curious, become teachable, and choose to change. We get to live with intent and purpose from this day forward. If you are not happy with your life and you want that to change, you have to be the one to change. Your willingness and courage to change make you part of the solution.

Chapter 2

HOW IT IS

Ask a cute little first-grader what she wants to be when she grows up, and she will come up with "chef," "teacher," and such. You never hear "drug addict" or "shoplifter." She isn't thinking that she could get hooked on alcohol or drugs when five years later she takes that first drink. She has heard all the propaganda about drugs being bad, or drinking being bad, but then she sees her parents drink and hears about her friend Suzie's older brother doing drugs, and he is just totally cool. The progression through adolescence for those who abuse drugs and alcohol is like a carnival ride that begins with a thrilling rise and dip of a roller coaster and leads to a nightmarish hall of horrors that has no exit.

The process of human development through puberty and into the teen years is awkward and disproportionate. Torsos and legs and hips and arms and faces progress toward adulthood seemingly out of sync for a few torturous years. Our brains develop as our bodies do, awkwardly maturing in different places at different times.

Here is a general description of adolescence as described by some of the young women I have interviewed. At about ten years old, most girls have bought in to the notion that they have to be popular to be happy. They need to belong, to fit in. They cannot tolerate being rejected. Peers are everything. Boyfriends are the symbol of acceptability. Having a boyfriend reassures the awkward adolescent girl that she is okay. Girlfriends are needed but not to be trusted. They see the models and the Barbie dolls and fear that if their awkwardly developing bodies aren't perfect, they will be made fun of by the other girls and they will never have a boyfriend. They have been bombarded with the message that the only way to attract a boyfriend is to be sexy. With their hormones raging and their undeveloped brains unable to keep up with the complexity of their new bodies and social demands, they start fooling around with oral sex first because they don't consider it "sex." They may start throwing up their food, thinking for a while that this is what it is going to take them to keep them thin and therefore attractive.

They fall in and out of love easily, and every painful moment feels like a life sentence of misery. They don't know how to cope, so they try drugs or alcohol to numb the feelings. It works for a short while, but then it doesn't, so they try harder. They become secretive and filled with self-loathing and don't even understand what happened. Their pain may be so great that they begin cutting themselves.

According to many of the young men who I have interviewed, adolescence is incredibly tough. The boys are a little slower to develop, so they watch girls who had been strong and smart in grade school now transform before their eyes and forfeit their power to other boys. Developing awkwardly and often later than their female peers, boys also fear social rejection. Compared to older boys, they are woefully inadequate. Feelings are considered weak and unmanly. They protect themselves by shutting down their feelings.

They, like the girls, fall in love easily but are more conflicted about relationships. They fear that the other boys will not think they are cool. They fear that they will be failures. They have to be tough and invulnerable. They cannot talk about their fear. Their hormones are enslaving them, and they begin to objectify women. Some use and abuse the girls and have no problem justifying their behavior because the girls allow it. If they show tenderness, fear, or even cautiousness, they may be bullied or humiliated. They have no idea what they are doing. They do things that they swear they will never tell another living soul. It feels like fun, and it feels normal, but it also leaves them feeling hollow and worthless.

Already highly emotional, both the girls and the boys become filled with fear and shame. They compare themselves to others, looking for validation, but some never receive it. Their peers are their world, and yet those peers are equally inexperienced.

If a boy talks to his parents about this feeling of anxiety, it's pretty likely he is going to hear how attractive or smart he is, but to him your opinion doesn't really count because you do not really know him the way his peers do. You will tell him that it will all be okay and that he shouldn't feel anxious. This is not helpful. Now he feels not only the shame and fear he had when the conversation began but also now feels inadequate because his parents have told him that he shouldn't feel what he is clearly feeling. He is alone. He can feel intense loneliness in the midst of a loving family. Peers become his lifeline.

The reason for starting to use drugs that is most frequently endorsed by adolescents is peers. They have a critical need for acceptance in a social scene that is bewildering, including peers who use drugs, peers who bully, and peers who reject and make fun of others. When asked where they feel the worst about themselves, it's school. When asked where they buy their drugs, it's school. Kids don't want their parents to know that they feel like social outcasts, that they don't have the skills to negotiate a terrifying adolescent culture. They are becoming adults. They are driven to seek the reassurance of belonging, of significance among their peers as they separate from their families. They are disengaging from their parents. They turn to their peers for answers, and their peers are just as confused and inexperienced as they are. Someone uses drugs or alcohol, and it ends up being a great solution. It works.

So teens try a drink or smoke some marijuana when it's offered by a "friend." It tastes terrible, but they can tolerate it. They feel relief from life's misery and their social fears. Nothing terrible usually happens that first time or two or three. They can leave it alone or drink or smoke marijuana only occasionally for a while. It doesn't seem so dangerous. The parents must be stupid or too old to know what they are talking about when they say that it's so dangerous. They rationalize when a friend gets sent away to treatment, "That kid's parents are crazy." They are pretty sure that "addiction" happens to other, dumb kids who can't handle themselves. For many, drugs are the answer to their social fear and numb their pain.

Our social structure is aligned around the myth that drug and alcohol use is most prevalent in disadvantaged groups. We stereotype by focusing on the stress of financial hardship, of having both parents out of the house at work, at having only one parent, and any of the variables that place us at risk for "bad" behavior as children. We believe that if we live in the right neighborhood, send our children to the right schools, and love them with all of our hearts, they will be immune from the evils of our crazy culture.

Many of us do not think our child is at risk. We do not see any warning signs. Our minds are resistant to any input that does not fit into our perception of who our child is. This is denial. We are shocked when we learn that our child has been drinking or smoking pot. Of course when caught, our child tells us that it is the first time. We explain the dangers, and our child promises to never do it again. We believe they won't. But they do, and we hold on to our denial and attribute their disturbing behavior to the ups and downs of the teen years.

How do we know when a teen's behavior is beyond the normal moodiness of adolescence? Drug and alcohol use is very typical teen behavior in our culture. Most of us just hope and pray that what our child is experiencing is a phase that will go away because we have no idea what to do about it. But here is the answer: without being redirected, they do not grow out of it. It doesn't matter what drives insolence, rudeness, lashing out, being manipulative, lying, or disrespect. We have to redirect the behavior even if they are just in a bad mood. Being a teenager doesn't justify bad behavior. Even if they are just smoking a little marijuana, it is important to shut it down.

If you are able to interrupt your child's drug or alcohol use early on, the likelihood of your child developing an addiction is greatly diminished (Substance Abuse and Mental Services Administration, 2010). For that reason alone, it is advisable for parents to take the matter seriously. Forget about the term *experimenting*. Many of us have used drugs and alcohol during our lifetimes and have had no real problems as a result. Parents who used drugs in their youth, or who continue to occasionally use an illegal substance and have not become dysfunctional, may find it difficult to take substantive action without feeling hypocritical. We will try to rationalize and be tolerant of a fourteen-year-old who is smoking marijuana or who has become sexually active, even though this child's brain is not even close to being developed enough to deal with the extent of damage that can come from this behavior.

By the time parents are convinced that their child has a problem, the teen has likely been using drugs for three or more years. Although rare, some teens report their first use of illegal substances at seven to nine years old. More typically, the vulnerable years are eleven to thirteen. The adolescent brain is incredibly vulnerable and cannot manage the complexity of their experience. The drugs feel great, but they have to alienate themselves from the adult world in order to use them on a regular basis.

Alcohol is the most widely abused substance among adolescents. In 2013, The National Institute on Drug Abuse's *Monitoring the Future* Survey indicated that 27.8 percent of eighth graders, 52.1 percent of tenth graders, and 68.2 percent of twelfth graders reported drinking alcohol. Young people drink less often than adults, but when they drink, they drink to get drunk. On average, teens drink about five drinks on any occasion, which is considered binge drinking.

Marijuana is the most widely abused drug among adolescents. In 2013, 16.5 percent of eighth graders, 35.8 percent of tenth graders, and 45.5 percent of twelfth graders surveyed in the NIDA study reported using marijuana in the past year.

Inhalants are more frequently used by twelve- to thirteen-year-olds. As the respondents' ages increase, the drugs of choice shift to predominantly marijuana and prescription drugs, with a lifetime incidence of use of illicit drugs at 50.2 percent of the population in the sixteen- to seventeen-year-old range. Ten percent of high school seniors report using Vicodin, and nearly 5 percent of seniors report using OxyContin in the past year. Eight percent of the population in the twelve- to seventeen-year-old range met the criteria for substance dependence or abuse for either illicit drugs or alcohol in the year 2013.

The Center for Disease Control (CDC) reports that every year in our nation, 3,000 teens die from overdoses, 3,627 teens attempt suicide, 815 are treated for self-inflicted injuries, and 1,695 commit suicide successfully (Miniño, 2010). According to the CDC, every year one in four teens seriously considers or makes a plan to suicide. Ninety percent of those who actually commit suicide have been diagnosed with a mental illness or substance use disorder. More teens die from drug-related harm than from motor vehicle accidents (SAMHSA). Children die every day, accidentally or by design, as a result of feeling the need to numb their feelings.

Teens lie. They lie to protect their friends, their culture, their privacy, their budding independence, and to some degree their parents. Parents find it hard to believe that their children would lie to them, but they do. They have just enough frontal lobe development to rationalize all of the arguments for why parents are wrong. They become masterful at pushing parents' buttons. The danger is thrilling. They feel tough, strong, and smart. They believe they are too smart to let drug or alcohol use get out of control.

But it does.

Chapter 3

ENTITLEMENT

··

I am, therefore I deserve.
—Entitled teen

··

As new parents, our first prideful comments are typically about our child's brilliance. We anticipate greatness in his or her future. We revel in our child's beauty. We are so in love that we are willing to do anything for this precious baby.

Our cultural thinking about the parent-child relationship is that if our children look good on the outside, we must be good parents. Our children reflect our value as parents. Of course this is ridiculous, but we buy into it, so our egos are wrapped up in making sure we do our job. We want to make sure that they look good and are successful, whatever that means. If they do, we must be okay. The barometer of good parenting is often only surface deep.

We make certain that they are in the best school we can find or afford. We want them to have wonderful things around them—the best toys, clothes, schools, etc. We enroll them in dance, soccer, basketball, art, and music classes almost at birth. We want to foster their skill development. We don't want them to waste their lives being bored. We don't want them to ever feel left out.

We want to keep them happy. We buy them things, take them places, and do all manner of things for them so that they will be happy. As parents, we *entitle* our children by teaching them that they deserve anything and everything we can give them or do for them, just because we love them that much. When they look good on the outside—meaning that they are happy, well-groomed, have good manners, and so forth—we assume that they have self-esteem.

We want them to have the things that we would have liked to have had when we were kids. We want them to not just understand our decisions but to buy into them. We hate to deny them anything, and when we do, we talk to them about it at great length, hoping that they will finally agree that we are doing the right thing. They do not. They ask, and we give. We entitle our children to our time, our money, and our tolerance of unpleasant behavior by giving them what they want *without any link to their personal effort*. They get things from us simply because they exist and because it feels good to give them things. We want to feel good about ourselves. We want them to feel loved and to love us back.

The child comes to believe that this is what we, as parents, are supposed to do. We are supposed to clean up after them, provide everything they want, and make special efforts to do whatever they ask of us. They have come to feel that their happiness is our responsibility because after all, we asked for this gig, and they didn't. We gave them everything they wanted when they were little children, but now their wants seem to be insatiable. When we are not forthcoming, they accuse us of being selfish. Their wants should come before all else. We hate arguments about this. We want everything in their lives to be fair. We feel that we have to make up for any disappointments they may have had in the past. We begin to feel guilty about having our own things without buying the equivalent for them. We may even sacrifice our credit and financial security to provide an indulgence for our child.

We have expectations also. They will have self-esteem. They will love and appreciate us. They will recognize that we give up our needs to take care of theirs. They will be happy and grateful. But it doesn't work that way. We feel good giving and doing for them, and they feel good receiving in the short run. They smile and are nice to us, but these good feelings are fleeting. They become entitled.

There used to be a reality TV show called *My Super Sweet Sixteen* that chronicled outrageously elaborate birthday parties thrown by super-wealthy parents. The parties become competitive, each having to outshine all others. The newly sixteen-year-old *prima donna* melts down over receiving the wrong color of BMW from perplexed parents, who wring their hands and say, "How can she be so unhappy? We have given her everything she could possibly ever want!"

Pretty soon our children have the expectation that not only we but others should do for them those things that they could and should do for themselves; they truly believe that they are owed special treatment. Entitled people's happiness is in the hands of others. They only feel happiness when their wants are fulfilled but quickly sink into emptiness. The frustration of unsatisfied needs and powerlessness to take charge of their own happiness is overwhelming. Entitlement and the chronic unhappiness it comes with are the direct result of indulgent parenting.

The state of entitlement precludes gratitude. We will never be grateful if we believe that the world is indebted to us. Humility is the antidote. Humility and gratitude cannot coexist with entitlement.

When we don't allow our children to earn their privileges, learn from failure, and experience discomfort, we rob them of the opportunity to develop qualities that will sustain them through life. They have no self-respect, confidence, gratitude, or empathy. They become resentful bottomless pits of need and expectation. There is never enough.

The entitled mentality assumes a level of deserving and power that is distorted by beliefs that deny the reality of their situation. Here are some examples that I have heard from teens in drug treatment:

- "If I don't take my medication, it's my mom's fault."
- "You can't take that away from me! It's *mine*!"
- "If she's stupid enough to leave her purse in sight, she deserves to have her money stolen."
- "There's no way I'm taking the bus. If you want me to go to school, you are going to have to drive me."

- "I'll agree to go to drug rehab/treatment but not until after the holidays."
- "I can't be in treatment on my birthday. That's not fair."
- "I was late because my mom didn't wake me up."
- "[with a mouthful of nuts and one hand in an open jar] Look what I found in your cabinet!"

Jim Fay and Don Billings, in *From Innocence to Entitlement* (2005, p. 6) describe it this way:

> Acting as an enemy of happiness, the entitled perspective justifies and even rationalizes dissatisfaction. Entitlement places a stamp labeled NOT ENOUGH over the lenses through which we view life.

Some teens learn their entitlement from entitled parents. Entitled parents make every effort to get something for nothing. Some parents feel that their success entitles them to pick and choose which rules to follow. I have learned much from adults who seek my professional services, plead for help, and insist that they get immediate attention but then are reluctant to pay the bill.

When we train our children that their happiness is achieved through looking good, having a lot of stuff, going to the right school, being smart, living in the right neighborhood, and being popular, and we go to great lengths to provide all of that for them, we are setting them up to suffer, with no tools to alleviate the suffering. This creates false pride—pride based upon qualities over which they have very little control.

Entitlement is a parasite that overwhelms its victims, tricking them into thinking they are owed. If my value is determined by what you provide, if it is tethered to you as my provider, then you are responsible for my self-esteem and my self-loathing, and I have no control and no responsibility. Just as the junkie developing tolerance wants more and then even more, the entitled child's wants become demands, essential for their few transient moments of reassurance that they have value. They need others to fulfill their needs, and yet they abhor needing anyone. I need you but I hate you. You have taught me that it is your job to make me happy, and you are failing. Really, I hate myself, but that's your fault. This is what I term *hostile dependency.*

We feel hurt or frustrated by the lack of gratitude that the teen shows. That frustration is a clear sign that you need to *stop.* Every unearned item further stunts his maturity. He cannot grow into responsibility if you do not allow it.

We see that we are failing as parents, and what is our first inclination? We do more. More of the same showering with hollow praise and privileges, until we get angry and criticize and shame them. They do not get better until we get better.

Self-esteem is based upon actions. We cannot develop self-esteem by simply being, taking, and receiving.

Self-esteem develops in tandem with integrity by finishing what we start, particularly if it's difficult. It comes from overcoming hardship, working through problems, from relieving others of the burden of doing for us what we have the ability or can learn to do for ourselves. It comes from acknowledging and accepting our mistakes and imperfections. It comes from allowing ourselves to love others without condition, from being of service to others.

The entitled individual is self-focused and cannot tolerate personal imperfections to the degree that they keep those imperfections carefully hidden from others. A person with self-esteem is other-focused, expects some hardships, and humbly embraces personal imperfections with courage.

We don't just "get" or "have" self-esteem any more than we "get" or "have" entitlement. We have to earn either of these qualities. To gain self-esteem from a position of entitlement, one must un-learn the entitlement attitude by engaging in esteem-able acts on a consistent basis.

One does not learn gratitude from abundance. Nor does one develop humility by avoiding failure. As parents, we can help our children through this process by allowing them the experience of hardship, failure, inadequacy, lack of preparedness, and all of those unpleasant times that shaped our own lives. We can empathize and cheer them on as they overcome the obstacles to maturity and self-esteem.

The most loving thing parents can do is to allow our children to grow strength and self-esteem by having to do their own work and earn their own things. It isn't easy to watch our child's discomfort and inevitable struggles and failures. True parental love is about not accepting behavior that dishonors our child's dignity, behavior that we know to be wrong.

We learn to say no. We create opportunities for our children to earn their privileges and possessions, and we hold them accountable to their commitments. We teach them and require them to clean up after themselves, to help with household duties, to do their own laundry, to give us ample time to plan if we are going to give them a ride somewhere, to do their own homework.

We don't always know the right thing to do in every situation, but we can pretty easily figure out what the wrong things are and avoid them. Never lie for or to your child. We make a strong and loving statement when we refuse to lie to the school to cover a child's absence. When they have to do additional work to get credit, they will understand that we are holding them to a standard that they will feel proud of.

Never reward your child for doing things that he or she should do anyway. It makes no sense to reward a child for making his bed, doing his laundry, etc. These are his responsibilities anyway as a member of the family whose developing maturity indicates that these chores are appropriate responsibilities.

For parents who have not used the word much, saying no can be difficult but life-changing. The teen will be angry. The teen might think we are being unreasonable. The teen might feel betrayed or might see our refusal as evidence of unfairness. We want our child to buy into our position. This is an unreasonable expectation and flawed thinking. If we fall into this trap, we start justifying our position and our child will argue every point and finally end with something about how ridiculous we are, how pathetic that we are letting some outside person talk them into behaving like tyrants. Do we not have our own minds? For some reason this argument touches us. Then we find ourselves in an argument about our incompetence.

The simple shift from being manipulated by our teen to allowing our teen to be responsible for earning privileges and material goods is essential and powerful. I have seen a family bail their son out of juvenile detention to join them on a family vacation. They, of course, were hoping desperately that he would be pleasant and that the vacation would be the picture of warm togetherness that it had not been for years. This was unreasonable to expect and of course extremely entitling for the boy. There was literally nothing he could do that would stop his parents from giving him more and more. He was of course ungrateful and actually blamed them for his bad behavior.

Those hours in juvenile detention are wonderful opportunities for him to look at where his choices are taking him. If you rush to bail him out, he loses that opportunity.

We don't like ambiguity and uncertainty. We really don't like the anxiety we see in our child when he or she is experiencing that kind of uncertainty. We want to rescue others from that feeling. This is actually cruel. When we interfere with the moment that might just create some ownership in our child's life, we are delaying his or her development and he or she will not have any idea how to cope as an adult. The anxious hours, wondering if and when you will be there, are the consequence of *his* choice, not yours. He wants the material comforts of home. He feels entitled to them. His material comforts are underwritten by your generosity. If he isn't grateful, it is because he is entitled. If he isn't grateful, it is because he has done nothing to earn these things and they therefore have no value except to feed his ego.

We don't have to justify our adult, parental decisions. When finally, our child has to face our refusal and is enraged by it, we have created a powerful, teachable moment. You are in charge, and you do have reasons that are not necessary to discuss. You can discuss your reasons if you want, but your child is not going to reply with, "Oh, now I understand." You can be sure that your child is looking for loopholes to goad you into an argument. Or, you can simply say no. If he or she argues or demands a reason, you have the opportunity to practice being both loving and firmly resolute. Of course, the adolescent does understand the reasons but knows that if he or she can goad the parent into a discussion there is still some possibility of getting to yes. A response like, "I am certain that you already understand this, and we can talk about it later if you would like, but my position is firm, and it seems like a waste of time to talk about it." These are precious opportunities for our children to experience us as adults, in charge, confident and yet loving, and for us to experience the relief of standing our ground without hiding behind anger. Even as the child stomps away, we feel stronger.

For those of us who are accustomed to using our anger to get our way, saying no is not a problem. The challenge for us then is to learn to say no with love and respect. We may have been using anger as a weapon to convey disapproval of the teen in general, which creates a chasm in the relationship that is very tough to bridge. When you refuse a teen's request, you can learn to deliver the message with the kind of respect that can serve as a model for your child's behavior.

Some of us find it easier to refuse our child's demands or requests when we are angry. Anger feels powerful, although if you rage at your child, you are no longer the adult in the interaction. We feel that we can hide behind anger when we feel fear, but it is ineffective. Don't rage. If you do, you have lost your power in the relationship and will become punitive and unreasonable. Your child will have learned that yelling at people is a reasonable way to deal with disappointment or frustration, to deal with feeling unappreciated, to deal with rejection, and you will potentially have taught him to become abusive or a bully.

Your child can earn privileges that require responsibility and trust by demonstrating responsible, trustworthy behavior. Do not give a car or allow driving privileges to a teen who is not respectful, trustworthy, responsible, and grateful. If you have already given the car to your teen and he or she is ungrateful and irresponsible, you have the right to sell the car. Then, if he or she wants a car it should be earned. Empower the child to earn his or her way, and he will be a grateful, mature adult in a few years.

Some additional recommendations:

1. You can defer any decision until you are comfortable with it by saying, "If you must have an answer this minute, the answer has to be no. Otherwise I need a little time to think it through (or talk it over with your coparent). I will tell you in the morning (or whenever)."

2. Never say yes on a promise. Your child is not likely to fulfill the promise. You have probably had or known of an experience when someone has paid a worker up front for a job that was never done. Your teen may have good intentions, but the promise will probably not happen.

Typical teen tricks to win (there are many—you have already heard them):

1. "I need this for my sobriety." A teen who is manipulating you with sobriety is making his or her sobriety your problem. It is not. His or her sobriety is his or her problem.

2. "I deserve to know your reason." When has knowing the reason made a difference to the teen? A teen is not going to be satisfied with knowing the reason.

3. "You allowed this for my siblings." Why would we want to repeat mistakes we may have made in the past just to seem fair? This argument would be funny if it went the other way.

4. "I will do it anyway. You can't keep me from it." The consequences of wrong behavior will be in place, and the teen must learn to take responsibility for his or her acts. You cannot stop him or her.

5. "You have been brainwashed by your sponsor [or that twelve-step propaganda, or your therapist, or someone who is in support of your changing attitudes]. Don't you have a mind of your own?" It's okay to admit to your child that the old way that you were dealing with things just wasn't working for you, and that yes, you are willing to consult an expert because your family is that important to you.

6. "I will relapse if I can't do this." Another example of the teen trying to blame his or her wrong choices on you. Don't buy it.

7. And the ultimate: "I will kill myself." Go straight to a hospital. See below.

For any of the first five, you will quickly get the hang of just saying that it isn't up for discussion. You may have to request that they leave the room, or you may have to excuse yourself and leave the room. Do not get drawn into a discussion. Do not capitulate. If you change your position, they will never learn this simple lesson. If they threaten relapse, offer to place them in treatment if they are so fragile.

If your child threatens suicide, *never* assume that it is a veiled threat. Take the teen to an emergency room and have him or her evaluated. You will spend a few hours together in the waiting room and eventually have a psychiatric evaluation. If your teen is actually suicidal, you may have saved your child's life and yours as well. If it was a bluff, you will have made it clear that you will take care of your child at any cost and do the hard things for his or her benefit, and your child is unlikely to repeat that threat in an effort to manipulate you.

Kids who are raised in a household that has been divided by divorce are often parented out of guilt. Each parent feels the need to be all things to that child because their decisions have robbed the child of the Norman Rockwell fantasy of a family of staying together and being happy for the rest of their lives.

Parenting out of fear and guilt is parenting out of distorted thinking. Parenting out of fear either motivates us to protect our child so much that they never experience any kind of pain, which we have talked about. Pain is important to growth. Parenting out of guilt is selfishly parenting out of what *we* need, wanting to reassure ourselves that we're doing everything we can do to deal with *our own feelings* about the decisions we've made.

When we divorce, we are still both the parents of our children, and we have to continue to parent our children together. Otherwise the children suffer tremendous confusion as they receive inconsistent messages and values. The children have characteristics of both parents and are therefore in danger of being the object of either or both parents' hatred. They become chameleons and feel the loss every time they have to leave one household to go to the other. We feel their pain and we want to make up for our selfish decision to divorce, so we do even more for them. They learn that they can use the situation to their advantage. They learn to play the game and placate whichever parent they are near. They use their parents' animosity toward each other so that they can get their way. They are doing what adolescents do. They want to feel good and will go to great lengths to do so. They become masters at triangulation.

You cannot be two parents. You cannot make up for the loss of one parent. You cannot undo the pain of divorce. These are experiences that children have. Do not deny your child the right to his or her own sadness. Empathize. It is sad for everyone when these things occur. Don't justify it or blame someone. These can be powerful experiences that foster wisdom or they can become the moment beyond which there is a darkness that makes it very tough to find one's way.

Chapter 4

THE BRAIN AND HABITS

....

The teen brain is often ridiculed as an oxymoron—
an example of biology gone wrong.
—Jay N. Giedd

....

When our kids do crazy things that baffle us, we are usually in such disbelief that we have no idea how to respond. We try to make sense of their behavior.

Smart, capable adolescents make decisions that are clearly self-destructive and have huge negative consequences. We warn them, and they do it anyway. Our adolescent kids are smart, but their behavior is not rational. We now understand the biology of the adolescent brain. They don't realize it, but they are making life-or-death decisions with a brain that is not even close to ready—a brain that, under emotional circumstances, reacts out of emotion and disregards logic. They just aren't yet capable of using logic to address an emotional issue.

For that matter, many adults do not acknowledge their ability to override gut impulses with good, logical decision-making either! People who are otherwise reasonable risk their lives and the lives of others when momentarily overwhelmed by road rage. Most of us can have feelings and not act. Some feel the emotion and cannot pause to control their response: they act and often regret it. When I began to study the brain, how it works and how it develops, I began to understand adolescent thinking.

Our brains are the organ in charge of every emotional, intellectual, psychological, physical, and spiritual aspect of our being. We think of thoughts, behavior, and our brains as distinct phenomena, but they are actually reciprocating, interactive functions. Further, each has the ability to change the others. Behavior changes our thoughts and the physical connections in the brain. Thoughts can motivate behavior and can change the paths of connections in the brain.

Changes in our brain produce changes in our thinking and our behavior. This organ, essential to life, is sometimes horribly abused by our kids and subsequently produces insane thinking and insane behavior.

A college student took ketamine, a powerful anesthetic, and was unconscious. Her friends did not know what to do. Someone gave her a pill and she took it, not even knowing that it was ketamine. I asked an anesthesiologist about it and she said, "Ketamine. Now there's a drug that no anesthesiologist would ever get hooked on. You might use it in a tranquilizer gun to shoot a gorilla running at you, but take it recreationally? Never. It would be a very bad experience." Its effects include abnormal heart rhythm, nausea, vomiting, excess salivation, and bladder inflammation. It will also put you to sleep and inhibit painful sensations, but it's a bad sleep with nightmares and disturbing psychotic experiences. This college student, whose success depends upon her brain, went to the emergency room because she had willingly poisoned the one organ that will determines every aspect of her being for the rest of her life, and there was never even a possibility of a pleasurable side effect. This is insane behavior and is often repeated.

There is useful literature on the web and in professional journals on the adolescent brain, and I encourage all to use those resources. The National Institute on Drug Abuse (NIDA—www.drugabuse. com), the Substance Abuse and Mental Health Services Administration (SAMHSA—www.samhsa.gov), and the National Institute of Mental Health (NIMH—www.nimh.nih.gov) have great information about teen mental health issues and substance abuse, including summaries of brain research. I summarize some of it here because it is so integral to understanding why our teens act the way they do.

How the Brain Communicates
Messages are carried within the brain and between your brain and your sense organs and muscles by a chain of signals along a series of string-like cells called neurons. A mosquito lands on your arm, triggering the neurons in your sensitive skin to fire. The message is carried from your skin to your brain and eventually back to your muscles so that you react. Each time one neuron passes on a signal to the next, the impulse has to be carried across a little tiny gap between cells called a synapse. The "sending" neuron releases a chemical, called a neurotransmitter, into the synapse, and the "receiving" neuron reacts to the chemical in the synapse, triggering the impulse to continue the message down the receiving neuron, and so on. The neurotransmitters in the synapse are then absorbed back into the neurons. Neurotransmitters are essential to every brain function and are the key to the effects of drugs in the brain. Drugs of abuse interfere with the normal functioning of neurotransmitters, disrupting, exaggerating, and changing the way our brains communicate.

Learning and Habit Formation
Experiences that are repeated over and over eventually result in automatic, unconscious habits, particularly in children and teens. We start with a first, possibly awkward experience that takes a bit of effort, as in learning to read or ride a bike. With repeated practice, our brain creates a bundle of connected memories that are very easy to recall. After a while, the memories of all of those related experiences are no longer conscious. Now we read or ride a bike without thinking about it. We are unaware of the processes that our brains have become trained to perform. This is how habits are formed.

This is the way we learn. Reading, balancing on a bicycle, playing a musical instrument, performing as an athlete, and driving a car are examples of learned, automatic processes. Other automatic processes are less obvious. Not just *what* we think, but *how* we think about people and experiences in our lives are learned automatic processes, based upon repeated personal exposure.

Memories that are associated with intense emotions, either positive or negative, are deeply imbedded and highly influential in the development of automatic processes and produce strong emotional recall when they are remembered even years later. We remember with great ease the events of special days in our lives. Most of us continue to prefer the music that we loved when we were teens, because those times were intensely emotional and the emotions were enhanced by the music.

We develop our individual patterns of being, believing, and acting in the world based upon our experiences throughout our early life. Learning has become knowing. It feels like truth, although it is just a habit of the mind, unique to each individual. All of the interactions in all of the relationships we have as we grow up come together to form the blueprint from which adult relationships are built. No two blueprints are alike. The relationship blueprint is powerful, regardless of the quality of the relationships that created it.

Unlearning takes as much effort as learning. You can unlearn your habits, whether they are psychological, emotional, relational, or physical. This is what it takes to change.

Adolescent Development and Brain Functioning

We used to think that after the initial growth spurt during infancy, our brains were pretty much complete and would not change again. Now we know that a second period of tremendous brain growth and change is in adolescence, which is defined by most researchers as the period between eleven and twenty-five. This second phase of brain maturation begins at about eleven years old, with the onset of puberty, and continues until complete, at about age twenty-four or twenty-five.

The process of maturation involves hormones and neurotransmitters, those chemicals produced in the brain that allow one nerve cell to communicate with another. When they are not functioning properly, we experience strange patterns of thoughts, emotions, and/or behaviors.

Several neurotransmitters and hormones are particularly salient to normal adolescence and are almost always affected by substance abuse.

- Dopamine affects movement and emotional responses as well as the experience of pleasure, pain, and alertness. Dopamine levels naturally decrease during adolescence.
- Serotonin is involved in emotional arousal, impulse control, anxiety, and mood fluctuations. Serotonin levels naturally decrease during adolescence.
- Norepinepherine affects alertness and arousal and interacts with dopamine in the reward system.
- Melatonin (a hormone, not a neurotransmitter) regulates the sleep-wake cycle. Changes in melatonin during adolescence result in an increased need for sleep.

Considered together, it makes perfect sense that adolescents are moody, sometimes gloomy, take risks, and have a hard time getting up in the morning. Dopamine is affected by essentially all drugs of abuse. Teens want to feel good. Drugs of abuse are very capable of making up for the feel-good neurotransmitters that are not quite producing as well as they will in adulthood.

In a fully developed brain, all segments can communicate with each other. This is not yet so for adolescents. Two major brain segments, the limbic system and the prefrontal cortex, are not yet communicating. The limbic system is the center of emotions. This is the area that is most affected by the onset of puberty—the area that is most directly influenced by the changes in neurotransmitter production that teens experience as their brain matures. During adolescence the limbic system rules. The emotion-producing, survival-reacting, pleasure-seeking, memory-making structures in the limbic system are in charge.

The frontal lobes of the neocortex provide "executive functions," which include analytic thinking, empathy, insight, goal-directed decisions, setting priorities, and all of those characteristics that a good manager uses to keep the workplace healthy. The frontal lobes are developing but cannot yet communicate with the limbic system. The neurons that connect the two develop throughout adolescence into an efficient pathway of communication by the midtwenties. Given an intellectual exercise in which an adolescent is asked what he or she would do if he or she were faced with some dilemma, the adolescent is likely to make as reasonable a decision as any adult. However, if presented with that same dilemma in real time under emotional circumstances, that rational frontal lobe decision is not going to be available. Further, *the teen's logical decision-making even when in a neutral environment favors fun over negative consequences.*

An adolescent is capable of making very logical arguments and can demonstrate complex analytical thought processes, until emotions are involved. The limbic system will overwhelm the teen. Thus, teen behavior is not always rational. It makes perfect sense.

In this way, risk-taking and impulsivity are biologically based in the developmental processes of the brain during adolescence. Emotion, pleasure, thrills, fun, drama—all driven by the changes in the brain during adolescence—serve the survival of the species through reproduction but not necessarily the survival of the individual.

A group of teens was shown a video that was intended to produce shock and fear along with an aversion to drinking and driving. One scene depicted a group of teens in a car, laughing and playing loud music, clearly under the influence of alcohol. Another scene showed a responsible teen driver, all passengers strapped in seatbelts, smiling and quietly driving calmly down the street. The responsible driver and his passengers all arrived at their destination. The other group of teens was shown after a deadly car wreck—spread out on the highway and in a ditch, bloody and disfigured, apparently dead. One of the girls I talked to later that day said, "But the drunk kids looked like they were having so much more fun!" Their logic is very different from adult logic.

Adolescents like activities that dump adrenaline, dopamine, and/or serotonin into the brain. This means action and/or drama. Sports are good, gossip is great, danger is better, sex is even better, but drugs really do the trick. Young people are tragically three times more likely to die between fifteen and twenty-four then they are between five and fifteen. It's not about character. It's not about being bad kids. They are children, being who they are biologically in a world that expects them to have controls that don't exist. *They need careful preparation and oversight.*

In spite of our warnings, lectures, and threats, there is little likelihood that the frontal lobes will magically connect and start rationally sending a *"stop"* signal to the limbic system. Kids tell me that they sometimes experience the fleeting thought, *I shouldn't be doing this*, at the same time they are engaging in something they shouldn't be doing. It rarely stops them. Parents need to serve as the executive in charge until the adolescent has the ability to manage independently. They can think like adults, they can learn like adults, they can talk like adults and certainly look like adults, but in an emotional situation, when the limbic system is most active, any similarity to adult brain functioning is lost.

So when you plan your perfect speech, the one that you are certain will transform your child, and it is a masterpiece of logic, compelling in its presentation of your position, and you deliver it with perfection, you will probably be very annoyed to find that it has zero impact. This is because you are operating under a premise that ignores reality. You cannot change another person by appealing to logic. The teen's brain doesn't function that way anyway.

Chapter 5

THE BRAIN, SUBSTANCE ABUSE, AND RECOVERY

....

Previously learned abilities to think logically and behave
rationally seem to have evaporated in a matter of hours.
—Ronald E. Dahl, MD
(Referencing *Romeo and Juliet* as an example of adolescent brain functioning)

....

Teens seek pleasure. They are fun machines. They are attracted to and engage in whatever activity will produce some dopamine and make them feel better.

Essentially all drugs abused by humans involve increasing dopamine levels in the brain. Dopamine creates pleasure. That sensation of pleasure and euphoria is encoded in the memory, and it tells the brain, "Wow, that was fun. It felt *great*. I think I should do that again." When you eat a pleasant meal, your dopamine levels elevate to about 150 percent of your normal state. People can become addicted to food and struggle throughout their lives to maintain a healthy weight. Sex increases dopamine levels by about 200 percent. People can become addicted to sex and ruin their relationships by seeking this pleasure. Daydreaming about food, sex, love, cocaine, or anything pleasurable creates an elevation in dopamine and thus a sensation of pleasure. People get hooked on preoccupation with these mental activities.

Cocaine use elevates dopamine by about 300 percent, and methamphetamine used intravenously elevates it by about 1100 percent. Even anticipating the reward elevates dopamine levels.

We know a lot of harmful stuff is going on in drug or alcohol abusers' brains while they indulge. Neurotransmitter receptors become less sensitive if repeatedly flooded with chemicals over time, so a subsequent dose of the same abused drug does not reach quite the same level of pleasure as the first. Seeking replication of that first experience of "super-euphoria," the user often increases the dosage. The circulatory system can become overloaded as the drug constricts vessels, requiring the heart to beat faster in order to oxygenate the body. The heart can rupture or vessels can tear. Neurons die out, and new connections cannot be formed. It takes up to a year without drugs or alcohol before the brain is completely free of the negative effects of drugs and alcohol.

Natural consequences take too long to deter most teens from an experience that promises excitement or pleasure *now*. Smoking tobacco is a good example. We know, without doubt, that smoking will kill you. It will turn your fingers yellow, cause your skin to wrinkle, damage your voice, and really smells bad to nonsmokers. Yet people smoke. It is addictive and very difficult to quit once hooked. It isn't about their bad character or their lack of willpower. They are addicted. There is nothing logical about it.

You may have been telling your children all their lives that there will be horrible consequences if they use drugs or drink alcohol. Then they do it, and their experiences are actually pretty pleasant. Harmful things can be happening in their brains, and their behavior can become reckless and dangerous, but they do not experience any negative experiences initially. They just feel good! They may drink too much and end up sick, miserable, and vomiting all night, but even this doesn't deter most teens from wanting to do it again. Obviously, they think, adults really don't know what they're talking about. It seems completely manageable to use drugs or drink alcohol until, for about 10 percent of the kids, it becomes unmanageable.

Their drug use may begin with an occasional drink or drug. It is pleasant. They know they could get caught so they become sneaky and private. This becomes part of the thrill. As they continue to use their drug, the effect is not quite as pronounced as it initially was. They begin to increase the frequency and amount that they use. They often try another drug.

Some become preoccupied with seeking the drug and neglect other activities they used to enjoy. They may use the drug more frequently and in larger quantities than they intended. They may get into trouble at school, at home, or even with law enforcement and continue to use the drug. They may lose some of their closest friendships and important relationships but continue to use the drug. They may find that if they discontinue their drug use, their bodies go into withdrawal, and they are miserable.

Under the influence of alcohol or drugs, the brain becomes less efficient in other areas as energy and attention are absorbed by the reward cycle. Positron emission tomography scans of people as they ingest cocaine illustrate visibly reduced brain activity (National Institute on Drug Abuse, 2015).

With prolonged use, the already compromised brain does not function well without the drug. Having become adjusted to the regular infusion of neurotransmitter-like substance, the brain is no longer producing the neurotransmitters that are available in sobriety.

The brain becomes habituated, dependent. The addict has progressed in his use to the point of needing the drug in order to function normally. While the addict continues to pursue the feeling of being high that used to result from drug use, he or she is now more preoccupied with keeping enough of the drug in his or her brain to avoid withdrawal and achieve something close to baseline brain functions. When the drug is no longer supplied, the body has to adjust to the scarcity and manifests physical symptoms. Just like we feel hunger when we haven't eaten, we begin to feel a craving for the drug. Our body has come to depend upon it. It is essential for functioning, as essential as food and water. The constant need to seek and use a drug, the physical effects in the brain, and failure to reach a desired level of euphoria typically lead to restlessness, irritability, and general discontentment. It is no longer fun. It is necessary and consuming.

The physical and emotional manifestations of withdrawal are different for the different drugs of abuse, but withdrawal is unpleasant, is often painful, can cause emotional upheaval, and in some cases can cause death. Withdrawal symptoms can last from three to ten days. The lingering effects upon the body and emotions can last six months. In the case of methamphetamine addiction, dopamine levels may never return to normal levels.

If you drink an abundance of alcohol, you are likely to have an unpleasant "hangover" as the substance is metabolized out of your system. If you smoke weed, you are likely to experience increased irritability the following day. These are effects of too much of a mind-altering chemical in the body. Impurities in alcohol are attacked by the body's immune system, resulting in flulike symptoms for several hours. Withdrawal is much more than this. Withdrawal is the result of having too little of a substance in a body that needs the substance to function.

Kids take drugs because they work. They successfully suspend their emotional discomfort (i.e., anxiety and fear). Some don't want to stop early on because they are having what they consider to be "fun" and later because they want to avoid withdrawal. Budding addicts who aren't very tolerant of the discomfort of a hangover will have another drink or another pill so that they can reintroduce the good feelings of the next drink on top of the bad feelings from the last one. Nonaddicts take this as a cue to not use the drug or drink again. With chronic use, the brain no longer heals between episodes and no longer reacts as strongly to the artificial substance ingested. So, the guy who can "really hold his liquor" is the one who has developed tolerance and needs to drink more than before to get the same perceived effect. The effects on the brain and body are equally damaging, but the individual's perception of intoxication is diminished. It isn't unusual for their peers to be unaware of the extent of their intoxication.

Once addicted, the consequences of drug or alcohol use have to be pretty huge in order to motivate an addict to attempt to stop using drugs or alcohol. Usually a person has to be miserable before they're willing to go through withdrawal. The withdrawal process leaves people's mood fluctuating so that they feel that they are overwhelmed while at the same time their heart rate and blood pressure are fluctuating. If they do manage to get through withdrawal, they are still addicted and thinking like a person who is addicted to drugs or alcohol. They do not know how to deal with life. Alcohol and drugs have become their sole tool for living, and they are no longer in control.

The effects of alcohol withdrawal are life threatening and must be medically supervised. Your brain regulates your whole body. It is used to alcohol. When you take it away, your brain chemistry tries to compensate. Your brain becomes very unstable. Your autonomic nervous system receives and sends contradictory signals, and your heart rate, blood pressure, and mood become erratic. You will be agitated. You may have alcohol hallucinosis in which you have transient auditory, visual, or tactile hallucinations (feel like your skin is crawling, etc.). You may have seizures or delirium tremens (DTs—confusion, fever, tremors, visual and auditory hallucinations, and rapid heartbeat). Withdrawal kills 1 to 5 percent of people who try to detoxify their bodies without medical help. Symptoms can begin to occur as soon as two hours after the last ingestion of alcohol, build for a few days, and then taper off. Although the acute withdrawal symptoms generally disappear after about a week to ten days, some symptoms can linger for as long as a year, primarily due to low dopamine levels, and are experienced as something like depression.

Withdrawal from the habitual use of marijuana produces irritability, sleeplessness, lack of appetite, and anxiety. The intensity of drug cravings during and after withdrawal from marijuana makes relapse very appealing. Memory lapses and reduced intellectual performance can last for many years.

If your body has become habituated to painkillers, the withdrawal effect will be pain. Your body will ache from the lack of naturally produced endorphins. You will have flulike symptoms, tremors, anxiety, nausea, sweating, moodiness, confusion, and headaches. These symptoms start slowly and build for several days, continuing as long as several weeks.

Most adolescents do not associate the feelings that are associated with their drug hangover as a consequence of their drug use. It feels as if their irritability, discontent, anxiety, and other emotional reactions are directly associated with their environment, including parents, siblings, teachers, and others who may question their behavior. Marijuana use is particularly difficult to live with because the irritability produces surly, disrespectful, and generally unpleasant behavior. Parents become concerned and usually more intrusive, thus proving the adolescent's attribution of his misery to his crazy parents. The solution? Get high again. The cycle repeats, and the result is chaos.

Recovery

Many teens quit using drugs well before they become addicted, but some cannot spontaneously discontinue their drug use, even when the consequences have become huge. They promise to quit and even believe their own promises. Teens typically need to be removed from their environment initially and to focus on nothing but their health and well-being, sometimes in professional treatment, to get their bodies through withdrawal, to begin to clear their brains, and to become educated about their disease.

The decision to stop using drugs or alcohol, once addicted, typically comes when an adolescent sees that he or she is out of control, life is unmanageable, and he or she needs help. At this point a teen is usually willing to do whatever it takes. This decision can be influenced by parents and by peers. The process of getting sober takes the consistent and relentless support of the people in the addict's environment. Support does not mean sympathy or making excuses for the addict.

The brain must be retrained, denial must be replaced with an honest and open assessment of reality, old habits must be replaced with new behavior, and old, dysfunctional self-concepts must be replaced with new and functional self-esteem.

Maturity, Mental Illness, Plasticity

One frustrating experience for both the adolescent and the parent is that the psychosocial maturity of the adolescent or young adult is stunted at the age of onset of drug and alcohol abuse. This phenomenon has been proved through research presented by Dr. Kitty Harris at Texas Tech University (Harris, 1983) and witnessed by virtually every parent and teen in recovery programs universally. The process of maturation resumes when the brain is free of drugs or alcohol and the adolescent has mature peers from whom he or she can learn. While arrested maturity wasn't scientifically understood until more recently, the literature used in twelve-step programs has validated immaturity as a common theme among addicts.

Maturing

In terms of age, most of us are fifteen going on thirty or forty or fifty. People in the program have observed that members stopped growing emotionally about the same time they started using mind-altering chemicals. It may sound funny, but these observations appear accurate. If we look around us, many newer members do seem stuck in their teenage years.

But abstinence, patience, and working the program help us mature to our proper ages. Given time, we can become the adults we have only pretended to be for so long. (Hazelden, 1998, March 28)

Another mental health issue associated with substance abuse by teens is serious mental illness. Neuroscientists are certain that substance use and mental illness correlate. Many mental illnesses first appear during the teen years, so the exact cause and effect is unclear. People with mental illnesses self-medicate with drugs of abuse. Do drugs of abuse stimulate the onset of serious mental illnesses that involve similar brain structures and chemicals? Clearly in some cases serious mental illnesses emerge during adolescent drug use and do not remit with recovery.

The plasticity, or adaptive nature of the developing adolescent brain, plays a huge part in the recovery process. Because the adolescent brain is developing along several lines that are not necessarily synchronized in a clearly understood way, medication management is often less effective than behavioral interventions. Adolescents can absolutely reinvent themselves if given the tools, and the changes can be lifelong. The earlier they begin this process, with the help of the family and a strong support system, the more likely they will be to experience lasting change.

Transitions

As one recovers, neurons that have been damaged begin to function normally about ninety to one hundred days after the last intake of a drug or alcohol. The potential for relapse is particularly high during this time. Even one hundred days post-cocaine use, the addict's thought process are not yet back to "normal." For this reason, when a teen is discharged from a residential treatment facility after thirty days, relapse is almost certain, even though the teen may genuinely have the intent to remain sober. A discharge at ninety to one hundred days is safer but must be managed carefully so that there is very little additional freedom introduced at any one time.

Each introduction of freedom requires that the teen learn how to deal with that freedom without the safety and restrictions of a more regulated environment. For this reason, each level of care needs to be introduced as the prior level is completed. While a teen is in residential treatment, in which the patient is housed under close watch, the family should create an aftercare plan. The aftercare plan should step down the intensity of treatment and restrictions as the teen adjusts and adapts the new habits to his or her life. Aftercare is the most critical and yet typically underutilized phase in the treatment of addictions.

Transitions from a facility to home typically require a change of treatment teams and ongoing outpatient therapy for a minimum of six months and preferably several years. Unlearning habits is a slow process of learning new behavior, developing skill at utilizing new tools, and establishing healthier substitute behaviors and healthy friends. Unless the teen and parent are being prepared for this from the first day they enter treatment, many families just go home thinking everything will be okay, and 85 percent relapse within a few months.

The Brain and Relapse

Substance abuse is the most costly health issue in our country. Recent estimates by SAMHSA place the annual cost in the United States of substance abuse and addiction at $600 billion per year. That is over $5,000 per household in the United States every year! Much of the cost is related to the morbidity and mortality of addiction but also to the chronic relapses that have come to be expected in the course of the disease.

Relapse appears to occur when a cue in the environment triggers a deeply embedded memory of drug use. Just as the smell of a favorite food, a television commercial, walking past the refrigerator, the sight of the cookie jar, photographs in a magazine, or the sound of someone nearby munching on a snack may trigger memories of eating that cause your stomach to rumble in hunger, drug-using memories can be stimulated by many cues. Each memory is associated with habituated reward pathways that anticipate the pleasurable experience of the drug by releasing dopamine, and the addict is enticed to drink or use a drug.

Memories of drug use are associated with almost every aspect of the addict's life. Those memories have been embedded as intensely emotional and satisfying. Thoughts of drug use are likely to produce some dopamine release, triggering drug-seeking behavior, behavior that has become habitual. Every friend, every emotion, every sound, every stick of furniture, every television show, and everything that was anywhere near his life at the time he was using can serve as a trigger, a cue for recall of the use, and thus produce dopamine release in the brain.

Preoccupation with the drug will subside over time. Because there are triggers everywhere that cue the addict to use, he or she will need to develop insight into the effects of his environment on his brain and thus identify triggers, so that he or she can avoid as much as possible the craving and automatic reactions that may be produced. Relapse prevention training is a part of most substance abuse treatment and effectively helps the addict identify those dangerous cues.

This does not always go away with time. Most people in recovery are urged to find new people, places, and things to replace their old relationships, hangouts, and activities. Teens must do this, and they need help doing it. This is a huge undertaking. The old friends cannot support the teen who is trying to recover. The old friends are either part of the problem or never used drugs in the first place. Our teens need kids who have been where they are and are willing to help and support them as they learn to live again. As new, intensely pleasurable memories are produced, the power of the old are diminished.

New, healthy, strongly emotionally laden experiences create memories to displace the drug-use memories. Physical exertion, intense and exciting social activities, and safe emotional risk-taking are effective at helping teens create new memories of healthy, happy experiences

The first five years of recovery are considered "early recovery" for the very reason that these years need to be filled with conscious effort to develop healthy habits of thought, emotion, relationship, and behavior. The old memories will remain but will hopefully become buried in a wealth of wonderful new memories, laden with fear, love, courage, vulnerability, gratitude, and self-esteem. The new memories have to be powerful in order to fulfill the necessary purpose of overshadowing the old.

Relapse is always possible. Some teens respond to relapse with renewed conviction that recovery must become their way of life. Some who relapse dive deeper than ever intended into the drug culture, seeking a euphoria that they can no longer find, deteriorating to harder drugs, higher doses, and riskier experiences. Some parents live in fear of relapse, knowing that the next time their child uses drugs may end his or her life. This is possible. Our fear will not prevent the relapse, and our vigilant monitoring of our child cannot prevent relapse. To talk about addiction as a "disease of relapse" sometimes helps parents deal with their fear. However, the best relapse prevention a parent can do is to stand firm in our conviction that we must hold our children to a standard that will honor them. We do this by creating clear boundaries, rules, and consequences, never enabling or entitling our child.

Sadly, relapse is inevitable if parents expect that a brief episode of treatment will "cure" their child.

The disease concept of addiction is resisted by some who feel that it lets the addict or alcoholic off the hook in some way. The last thing we want to do is let them off the hook. They have a potentially fatal illness that will kill them if they are not actively engaged in their own self-care. Unfortunately, there is such stigma associated with drug and alcohol addiction that many who are afflicted feel that they need to hide their recovery. They are then carrying a secret that makes recovery more difficult. If fear and shame are at the root of the addiction, it is extremely difficult to negotiate the unlearning of fear and shame in an environment that requires the denial of very salient aspects of oneself due to the fear of consequences and shame of being judged.

Adolescents are doing what they do in a culture that is pretty tough. We need to be there to help them negotiate their way. We set the standard for our children. When we let problem behavior slide, hoping it will self-correct, we lower the bar for them, crippling their ability to grow up. Tomorrow it will be worse because there were no consequences for today.

We need to stand firm for what we believe is right, and we need to set the limits that they are incapable of setting for themselves.

Chapter 6

WHAT TO DO ABOUT PEERS

....

Hang out with people better than you ...
and you'll drift in that direction.
—Warren Buffett

....

Human beings are pack animals. We function better when we are part of a tribe, clan, family, or community. Banding together, we adopt similar habits, beliefs, behaviors, and attitudes, which become the norms of the group. For new people to be accepted by the group, they have to adopt the norms of the group or have such a profound impact on the group that everyone in the group conforms to the new person. This is peer pressure. In all cultures, the norms of behavior in a social community create pressure for conformity. We become similar to the people with whom we identify. Our choice of groups, then, determines to some extent the direction of our lives.

The need to belong—to a social group and to a family—is so profound that the fear of being alone and unloved can drive self-destructive behavior. For some adults, it is unthinkable to walk away from a destructive relationship. Teens will risk being harmed to avoid rejection. Many of us find it difficult to assert differences of opinion from a group with which we identify.

When we decide to work on or change some important aspect of ourselves, we find people with that quality and join another group. Students who hang out with really good students are likely to study harder than those who hang out with friends who blow off school, play hard, and cram at the last minute. If we want to become better tennis players, we need to play with people who have more skill. We need people who have the qualities to which we aspire if we are interested in becoming better at anything in our lives.

When we need help but don't feel understood in our group, we get lonely. We can be lonely in a room full of people, in a marriage, or with our families if we are out of sync with the others. It can be very lonely to feel that we are the only parent whose child is out of control. We are overwhelmed with needs and feelings that are not experienced by members of our group, and they can't effectively respond. We don't necessarily want another group of friends, but we need people who can really relate to our experience. Friends may sympathize and are well-meaning but do not have the grasp on solutions, whereas those solutions are normal experiences in a group of parents who are in recovery with their teens.

Teens' need to belong is biologically driven and tends to take precedence over all other needs. Their friends help them establish their uniqueness and help them differentiate from their family members. Teens' friends help them figure out their morals and standards of behavior. To a teen, peer opinions and relationships become the focus of their world, often leaving parents feeling abandoned or rejected. The teen doesn't see it that way. They take their parents' love for granted, and they now have a totally new world to negotiate and master. They don't tell us much about that, and we therefore can't quite relate to their experience. They end up feeling lonely even in the family who loves them.

Substance-abusing teens hang out in groups whose shared purpose is to use, supply, condone, or at least turn a blind eye to their drug use. They experience dangerous escapades together, take risks together, share secrets, and know the relief that each other finds in their drug. These shared, highly emotional experiences create powerful memories and the illusion of true friendship. They understand each other. They become more secretive. They think they are invincible and that all of the messages about the dangers of drug use are propaganda. We think they are being "normal" teens. Both parent and child are in denial. Ultimately we feel increasingly alienated from them, and we start looking for solutions.

Invariably our first plan to regain our relationship with our child is to get him or her away from the influence of those bad kids. Many parents try the geographic cure, hoping that a new school or a new neighborhood will return our child to his or her former self. This won't solve the problem, unfortunately, because it isn't just the friends—your teen and his or her relationships with you and the rest of your family are now part of the problem. If you take away access to old friends without a very attractive and immediately available substitute peer group, the situation may get worse instead of better. Imagine the teen's friends as the trapeze that suspends him or her above a chasm of loneliness and misery, with no net. You can't expect your teen to let go of the trapeze and just hang there in midair until the next trapeze appears. Most likely, he or she will fall into the depths of misery. To our dismay, when we disrupt their friendships, our teens become more miserable and more withdrawn and ultimately end up seriously depressed or making new friends who seem to be clones of the former. The teen will gravitate toward the familiar: the drug-using kids who are immediately accepting as long as you get high and the substance that has in the past provided relief from misery. We are doomed if we try to come between our teen and his or her friendships. Peers are part of our teen's identity. Teens trust their peers and if they are abusing drugs or alcohol, do not trust their parents.

Because they desperately need to belong, it is critical that our teens find a group to which they can connect but that supports healthy behavioral norms. As frustrating as it is, we simply cannot choose our teenager's friends. If we do, we undermine the whole developmental function of the peer group as a tool for the teen's developing self-image. If I choose my child's friends, those friends are going to reflect my values and beliefs. They can't help our teen figure out how he or she is the same or different from us or anyone else. Many of us try to get our kids involved in our places of worship, under the assumption that those kids are all healthy. This usually doesn't work. Kids who are in trouble behaviorally will not relate to someone who has not been in trouble. Our teen may try to placate us by going along with our plan but will find at least one kid in the youth group who is there for the same reason, and they will end up getting high together. Or our teen may be that rare person whose "different" behavior compels the whole group to change.

Kids who have never been in serious trouble have a hard time understanding the troubled teen's choices. A teen who has been part of the drug scene can easily manipulate a normal teen because the normal teen doesn't recognize the depth of dishonesty and manipulation going on. *The best group for a teen in trouble is a group of teens who have been in trouble and have found their way out through healthy choices.*

This happens when the teen becomes really sick of being in trouble, of fighting with family members, of taking a path that invariably will lead nowhere, and chooses to go a new direction. The recommendations made in the remainder of this book will help parents create the opportunity for this to occur.

There is a very effective model for teen peer support that was developed in the early 1970s in Houston, specifically designed to provide that attractive alternative. It is called the Alternative Peer Group (APG). Imagine a group of sober and healthy teens who …

- reach out to each other for help and to offer love, encouragement, and healthy suggestions.
- are committed to recovery from self-destructive behaviors and substances.
- hang out together every day after school (or at school).
- spend every Friday night and all day Saturday together having more fun than they could have ever imagined.
- have parents who are all friends and talk to each other openly and regularly.
- express gratitude for all that they have in life
- enjoy their parents.

- are honest and look adults in the eye with a smile.
- do not play mind games.
- choose real talk over drama and gossip.
- can hear feedback from others, examine their part in any situation, and will admit their mistakes.
- understand that in order to develop self-esteem, they have to do things that are worthy of esteem, like honor commitments, finish what they start, and offer service to others.
- are committed to an ongoing relationship with a higher power.

These teens and their parents comprise an Alternative Peer Group (APG).

APGs are organizations that provide a healthy twelve-step-based community with positive peer accountability for teens and parents who need help. APGs are committed to maintaining adolescent and parent communities with social norms that promote character development. While other twelve-step organizations offer meetings and a participant-volunteer structure of sponsorship and leaders to provide mentoring and some accountability, the APG has talented and well-trained staff who oversee the volunteer structure, guide the daily activities of all of the participants, and establish strict standards with accountability to those standards.

Recovery communities are not new. There are many varieties of twelve-step programs in communities that are very helpful for adults. However, for teens to engage and stay, and for the parents to reunite and heal the family, the community has to be composed of families, not individuals, and above all, they have to be welcoming, outrageously fun, and attractive to both the teens and the parents. Mendizza (2004) describes the importance of "fun" in the optimal environment for healthy growth:

> Play is the optimum state for learning, performance, and well-being, the essence of education, and parenting ... (p. 113)

The APG is not treatment. The APG is the tribe within the greater community that sets the norms and standards for daily life. They have twelve-step meetings for both parents and for teens at least weekly, social activities for the teens on Saturdays, and regularly scheduled parent/teen activities. There are some APG organizations who offer counseling services, while some work with counseling professionals and facilities in the community. Some have or are affiliated with sober schools, some offer daily supervised after-school hangouts, some offer extensive outdoor adventure learning activities, some offer parent retreats and workshops, and some provide support for both adolescent and young adult communities. All APGs teach us to approach relationships with love, how to laugh at our crazy thinking, to let go of our illusion of control over others, and to play.

In an APG, a troubled teen can get sober in a community of teens who have been through what they have been through and have turned their lives around. Parents find a strong system of support among parents who have experienced a similar nightmare and have learned effective ways to parent their teens and to be supportive of each other.

New families get started when either the parent or the teen shows up at a meeting, and eventually the rest of the family follows. Sometimes the teen finds the group before the parents, and sometimes the parents find it first. Most teens don't want to walk into a room full of strangers. Most parents don't want to walk into a room full of strangers. Neither wants to if they think they are supposed to be talking about their problems with these new people. It isn't easy, and it takes courage. The nurturing, welcoming experience of walking into a room filled with people who have been where you are and know the pain and fear that you are experiencing is critical to their safety and willingness to return.

When families come into the APG, the teen sees other teens who are happy and who have great relationships with their parents. Most of the newcomers yearn for that kind of relationship and that kind of family. They do not believe that their family will ever become that open, that honest, and that happy. They do not believe that they themselves will ever have the kind of courage it takes to have an honest conversation with their parents. Most teens are amazed and excited to hear other teens talking about their real feelings and struggles right out in the open and loving each other. Most of them have never heard anyone talk honestly about their lives.

Most parents feel tremendous relief when they find their way to one of these groups. They have hope. They, like the teens, see parents who can talk openly without shame, can laugh at their mistakes, and who have loving relationships with their teens.

Kids need fun … and so do the parents! Traditional treatment is often all serious and hard work and can drive the teens away with the expectation of a terminally boring life without the use of chemicals, and it barely scratches the surface with the parents. Most of the adolescents who cross the doors into an APG did not learn how to have healthy fun as teens. They learned about the excitement of danger and the thrill of being introduced into a world that is completely foreign to their parents. That was fun. But that kind of fun led them into a hellish nightmare from which they could not awaken. Getting into trouble became a norm, and they developed a reputation among other parents as a bad kid. They came to expect adults to react negatively when they walked into a room.

In this group of new friends, there is no history. They are starting fresh. They don't have a reputation, and the parents aren't shrinking in horror as they walk through their homes. But they also can be who they really are. They don't have to keep secrets about the mistakes they have made, the risks they have taken, or the lengths they have gone to try to feel something other than pain. The other kids have been there, have found their way out, and are having more fun than the newcomer could have imagined.

Most of the teens begin to act better right away (except at home, where the history and emotional habits still haunt all of them). Hands down the most healing activity I have ever seen is an APG's softball tournament in which encouragement, enthusiasm for showing up, cheers for making the effort, and good sportsmanship created an atmosphere in which families were practicing behaviors and attitudes that reduced the friction in their homes. The APG staff must be talented people who have the ability to attract the family members with their joy and enthusiasm, and to hold their respect with their maturity and healthy choices.

The incoming teen has to be immersed in a positive culture for a significant period of time before beginning to trust even the healthiest of peers. The incoming parents slowly become comfortable talking honestly about their lives, taking ownership of their contribution to family problems, and quit blaming, taking things personally, and being in the victim role.

Giving up drugs is tough, but most of the kids want what the teen recovery community has. They may lie and manipulate for a while. They may secretly be getting high when they aren't around the group. They may get caught. The newcomer may relapse several times before he or she is able to fully commit to sobriety. This community is both loving and intolerant of drug or alcohol use. If they value being part of the group, they have to get and stay sober.

Some teens are not willing to engage in the new group, but the parent continues to participate. This is really important. The parents demonstrate what it looks like to follow through, work a program of recovery, finish what you start, learn how to treat each other with respect, admit their mistakes, and take care of themselves, and they no longer let the teen run their lives. Their marriages heal, and they establish hard limits for behavior in their homes, creating uncomfortable consequences for their teen's bad behavior.

If parents do not stay involved, the opportunity to come together as a family in recovery while their teen is still living at home will be lost. When parents do not participate in the community, their teen rarely stays in recovery. When the teen does stay but without the involvement of the parents, the teen emotionally outgrows his or her parents and ultimately has a limited adult relationship with them.

Slowly the teens begin to experience what self-esteem really feels like—through practicing honesty, commitment, and selflessness within their peer group. Parents learn the value of holding firm and appropriate standards for family members. They no longer use their parental position to try to manipulate or control their teen but find true parental power as they apply loving accountability in their relationships with children, guiding them with love and allowing them to learn from mistakes.

As families gain knowledge, experience, and strength, the chaos in the home subsides. The parents learn to establish themselves once again in the parental roles in their homes. They help each other solve parenting problems by sharing their experiences and remaining open to the ideas of those who are more experienced. They learn to unconditionally accept each other while discouraging unhealthy parenting.

Parents and the teens learn to admit their mistakes and listen to the feedback offered by their peers and each other. They learn to be the adult that they want their child to become. As the teens realize that they aren't the center of the universe, which is not an easy feat, they begin to form a concept of a power greater than the self.

They (parents and teens) then become mentors to incoming families who are in the thick of despair and confusion. New families come in, assimilate into the positive culture, learn from their mentors, develop the strength and wisdom they need, and give back by mentoring others and taking leadership roles in the group. This service function is very important to recovery. It keeps us humble and grateful, keeps us learning from others and continuing to grow, supports our personal accountability as we listen to our own words as we give advice to others, and offers the solidifying of knowledge that occurs when we teach what we have learned.

Families continue their involvement for between eighteen months and three years. There are few programs in the country that provide this, but this is what works. Recovery has to become a way of life, not a temporary stint before we return to our old and sick lives.

If you cannot find an APG, contact the Association of APGs, which can be found at www.aapg-recovery.com. If there isn't one in your area, perhaps you can start one. You will need some donated space, a few young people who are experienced (more than a few years) in recovery, a few adults who are experienced in Al-Anon (more than a few years), and a whole lot of willingness and energy. The group will need a talented and enthusiastic leader who can teach both teens and parents to lovingly hold each other accountable, to find fun and excitement in healthy activities as an alternative to drug use, and to organize opportunities that organically create the space for all to begin to laugh and play together as families. If you don't have access to an APG and can't yet start one, then make every effort to form an alliance with the parents of the teens in your child's world. Before you do that, learn as much as you can about the healthy peer culture that is possible.

Teens need a strong leader who has been in recovery for at least five years, is willing to spend fun time with them, and also has zero tolerance for self-destruction. This seems obvious, but I have seen countless counselors and teachers and even policemen get soft and let the child have one more chance, keep secrets from the parents, and even turn a blind eye to a teen's unhealthy choices. They aren't bad people, but in their effort to avoid "hurting" the teen, they undermine him and prolong his sickness. This person will not gain the respect of the teens. The group becomes a sham under a leader who is willing to excuse self-destructive behavior. The standards of behavior must be high. Often, teens who do not respond to traditional therapy or treatments will learn and grow from other teens through carefully designed and skillfully facilitated activities.

The remainder of this book is focused on the parenting skills that are taught in this kind of recovery community, necessary for the family to emerge intact from the nightmare. As the codependent literature says, the parents didn't cause the problem and can't cure or control it. However, we can sure learn enough to quit being *part of* the problem.

Therapy is by definition an activity that is intended to remediate a negative or unpleasant condition. Fishing can be therapy. A bubble bath can be therapy. Rock-climbing, mountain biking, yoga, walking, talking to a friend, petting an animal, playing softball, praying, and writing are all potentially therapeutic experiences.

Most of the teens who walk into my office do not trust a soul. They don't trust their parents, and they don't trust most of the kids they hang out with. They don't trust me. Why should they? Peers in middle school and high school can be mean and backstabbing, betray confidences, and use their vulnerabilities to hurt them. In fact it is this peer rejection and bullying that in many cases precipitates the initial use of substance for teens. One young woman tells her story:

> I thought I was fat when I was in fifth grade and found that I could throw up and not get fatter. Eventually I was both anorexic and bulimic because I would starve myself, and then if I broke down and ate, I would throw it up. One kid found out and told another, and they told another, until pretty much everyone knew. Kids would come up to me and call me a freak. Sometimes they would say things like, "Do us a favor. Just go kill yourself and get it over with, you freak."

She started cutting, became deeply depressed, found and used drugs heavily, and had a very serious, near-fatal suicide attempt before she found her way to an APG at fifteen. She graduated from the APG group and a sober high school three years later, all smiles and love, filled with self-esteem and gratitude for her life. She continues to mentor (sponsor) teen girls.

Chapter 7

FINDING YOUR POWER

....

The secret of change is to focus all of your energy, not on
fighting the old, but on building the new.
—Socrates

....

What we know is that parents have to *be* the person that they want their child to become and clearly hold them to that standard.

When the dark cloak of self-centeredness, misery, and self-destruction descends upon our child, some of us lower the bar, hoping that our child simply survives. When we lower the bar, we begin to tolerate behavior that is beneath the child's dignity. We give up on our standards. This sends the message that we do not believe they have the ability to do better. I heard one parent remark, "We had a good day today. She didn't call me obscene names even once."

The problem with this is that, unless held to a standard that honors their dignity as human beings, our children will have a tough time identifying, much less emulating, honorable behavior. This is easy to say. It feels overwhelming to implement any kind of parenting initiative that will help a teen who is out of control, rude, manipulative, hateful, and self-destructive. We feel like we have already tried it all.

It is baffling that our child seems to have so little character. We have always been kind and generous, so where is his or her kindness and generosity? We are not cruel to others, so how can he or she be so cruel? We feel totally powerless. A teen will not develop character by being told about it. Words, lectures, threats, and pleading will not affect the teen's behavior much. I have had the privilege to work with many families who have become stuck in this quagmire. As parents and sometimes as friends and spouses, we try to convince our loved ones that they should be grateful, loving, or happy by laying out a convincing argument. In a moment of clarity, one father finally exclaimed, "I can't argue her into happiness!"

People develop character through example and accountability. Of course, we feel that, as parents, we have provided that example and we have certainly let them know when they offended us. However, we react to our teen's lies and sneakiness by snooping and spying on them. We get sneaky, looking for evidence of something concrete with which to confront them. We may know that they are being dishonest, but we are not willing to challenge them without hard proof. We are not being honest and up front with them.

Teens whose parents try to manipulate them see the hypocrisy. If we cannot face those hard conversations, we will have a child who lies or otherwise avoids hard conversations. If we cannot admit our mistakes and acknowledge when we are wrong, our teen will not be able to admit his or her imperfections, mistakes, and bad choices or even look at himself. Helping a teen who is out of control requires that we first take a look at ourselves. It isn't easy to identify areas in which we need growth, but we can all always continue to grow emotionally.

Most of us think that because we don't do drugs and because we are productive and responsible that the problem is the child's, not ours. Okay, we can start there. We have a child who has a problem, and that is a problem in itself. We want the child to prosper. We want the child to love himself as we love him. We want our child to develop the humility and gratitude it takes to mature into an adult. We want all of these things and are frustrated by our powerlessness to effect any positive change in our child. This is our problem. We can only solve this problem by thoroughly and deeply examining our approaches to our family relationships.

It is unreasonable to expect a teen to change his or her behavior if we are not willing to examine behaviors and attitudes that we need to change in support of a healthier family. It takes courage, and it also takes humility. Eventually, we accept that we are human, we make mistakes, we learn, we grow, and we still make mistakes. We must begin to focus less on trying to fix our child and more on our own character: honesty, humility, consistency, commitment, respect for self and others.

Dishonesty is probably the largest source of discord and dysfunction in a family. As human beings we get so used to telling abbreviated, enhanced, distorted, or completely made up versions of the truth throughout our lives that we lose touch with how much and how often we are dishonest. We lie to ourselves when we rationalize our mistakes and blame others. We lie to ourselves when we refuse to see the reality of our family's dysfunction, when we "cover" for our loved ones because we don't want to admit that our family is in trouble. We lie when we pretend to be someone we are not or pretend that our children are perfect because they are not. We let our egos drown out any humility that may appear. We become perfectionistic and cannot admit wrongdoing.

Let's look at lying. We lie when we make commitments that we do not keep. We lie when we make excuses for our unhealthy choices. We lie when we keep silent because we are afraid to speak up. We lie when we keep information to ourselves in order to feel powerful. We lie when we omit information or distort the real story in order to avoid consequences or to manipulate another person. We lie when we withhold information because it might be difficult for another person to hear.

Perfectly rational, intelligent, and successful people may carefully craft their words and distort the truth to create the outcome they want. This is manipulative and dishonest. Behind every lie is ego. Every lie is self-serving. Without humility, the ego becomes fiercely self-protective. Our egos urge us to believe that we have the answers for other people's lives. We don't.

Most parents want humility and an acknowledgment of wrongdoing from a teen who has been caught being dishonest. The only way back from dishonesty to credibility is humility. We teach humility to our children by functioning with humility. It is a powerful thing to admit to a teen that you have been dishonest and you want to set things right. They need to see this vulnerability in you. Our vulnerability is a source of our strength, and yet we hide it as if it were shameful.

When we fail, we have reasons. We can rationalize being dishonest, trying to manipulate others, blaming others for our life choices, undermining our partner, and breaking promises. Reasons are just excuses to justify our failure and to protect our egos. Regardless of our reasons, we are still dishonest, manipulative, disloyal, and undependable. We grow when we face this truth. How many times have you heard excuses from your child? Have you not heard your child blame someone else for his or her problems? Those explanations and excuses are disappointing. Just once, would you not love to hear your child take full responsibility for his mistakes or problems, and express willingness to go to any length right the wrongs?

Sources of Power	Sources of powerlessness
Honesty	Lies/rationalization
Self-honesty	Denial
Ownership	Defensiveness/blame
Humility	Judgment/arrogance
Vulnerability	Pretending/faking It
Straightforwardness	Manipulation
Honoring commitments	Inconsistency/deviousness
Self-love	Insecurity

We have to be the person we want our child to become. All we can offer is our experience, our love, our personal insights, and our example. Unsolicited advice is rarely welcome. Logical arguments do not impact anyone's behavior. Honesty, straightforward conversations, ownership of our errors, humble amends, and gratitude for the bounty we enjoy are powerful. Excuses, blaming others, lies, and entitlement are our attempts to shield ourselves from reality, and keep us powerless.

When we take complete ownership for the state of our life and relationships, we are being honest. Personal growth begins with self-honesty. Brad Blanton calls this "radical honesty" and has written a great book about it (Blanton, 1996).

This is a path to strength in the family and to freedom from shame. We may not get our way, but what we end up with is so much better. We feel peace and have healthy relationships. We get what we need, not what we have attached ourselves to thinking we need.

It is the most amazing experience to see a kid watch the changes in his or her parent and see the lights go on in the kid's eyes. Mom and Dad are actually human beings who have feelings and are imperfect, who can admit it and are safe to talk to. Then the kid says something thoughtful or kind to the parent and the parent begins to understand that by doing these simple things, being honest and open, not allowing a person to mistreat us and not mistreating others, the whole family begins to heal.

Consistency is actually very closely aligned with honesty. Consistency is about being the same person in all situations. In other words, being the real you. I find it hard to trust a person who plays to the crowd, changing beliefs and taking different positions depending on what might be popular with the current audience. Inconsistency undermines trust.

This does not mean we don't have ups and downs, or that we don't adjust our behavior for various roles in our lives. It means that we are not trying to manipulate anyone into thinking that we are something that we are not. No impression management. The ego sets lots of traps for consistency. It is very difficult, when we are operating out of ego, to be honest and consistent about who we are. In other words, if we spend a lot of time worrying about what people think of us instead of being ourselves, we send mixed messages and no one knows what is real and sometimes we don't either. There is no need to hide our fears, insecurities, hopes, joy, and imperfections or any part of our humanness. We have all of those things. All of us. It's just fear that prompts us to pretend we don't.

I sometimes hear a person defending his or her problematic behavior by claiming, "This is just the way I am!" This thinking forecloses on our ownership of our lives. It is not the way that we are. It's the way that we have become. Through our experiences and our interpretations of them, we have been creating neural networks, forming new connections within a vast network of possibilities, storing away chunks of memory, essentially programming our brains to fire in certain ways. These patterns become habit. We can change them if we are aware of them.

We do have the ability to override habitual behavior, but it requires that we consciously attend to our behavior and *consciously* select a new response in the place of the old ones that feel "normal" for us. This is the heart of therapy. What am I doing that isn't working? What could I do instead? How do I do that? The new behavior feels awkward. If repeated enough, the networks will change and connect to create the new habit in place of the old. In this way our actions and our chosen thoughts make changes in our brains.

We need other people in our lives to help us see ourselves and our behavior accurately. Our brains are not going to generate new options for healthier behavior because we are already using the best thinking we can come up with. We can be open to new thinking and can change our patterns based upon the advice of a trusted friend, a therapist, self-help literature, and even by watching others who are functioning a little better than we in some areas.

Changing the way that we think, or the way we respond to the world, requires that we change the way our neurons fire. We have to practice. It feels awkward. We have to create new connections among neurons that have become habituated in old patterns. Then we have that moment of clarity. We have that great moment when the connection occurs and we have a new way of seeing things or a new piece of learning that will become part of our ongoing thought processes, just like that first gleeful moment when we balanced our bicycle and rode without wobbling and falling. In this way, our actions affect our thought processes, which actually change our brains, which is the source of our thoughts. It is a fascinating dance of reciprocal causation between brain, mind, and body that continues throughout life. Our brains are the source of our consciousness, and our consciousness can change our brains. Our behavior changes our consciousness and our brains. It is most effective to change behavior, which allows us to think a new way.

Early in my adulthood I came to the conclusion that I needed to redirect my life. By working with a skilled and patient therapist, I finally had that "Aha!" experience. I could not get where I wanted to be by hoping that someone else would do it for me. I had to create the life I wanted. I had to create the life I wanted by becoming the person I wanted to be. If I am a victim, I am powerless to run my own life. Victim thinking had to go.

Behaviors can change the way we feel. If we smile, we will feel better. If we say no even when it feels awkward but we are sure that it is the right response, we will feel empowered. If we do good things, right and just things, we feel good about our choices. Our actions can change the way we feel and think. Changing our thinking can also change our behavior, but the process requires much more effort and intent. When life is not working the way we want, we need to DO something different. We need to get off of autopilot and consciously pursue the life we want. We will not get there by waiting for someone else to do it.

If it was easy to change behavior, everybody would go to the gym every day, nobody would smoke, and all persons would eat healthy food. It's very difficult to change behavior patterns. People make millions of dollars trying to make it easy or even possible for people who feel hopeless to change a habit. It is not easy, but it is possible.

Chapter 8

CODEPENDENCY

....

Place the oxygen mask over your own face before
attempting to place it on your child.
—Airline attendant

....

I have heard people describe their codependency as an addiction
to another person. I have felt it that way myself. The objects of our
codependency consume our thoughts throughout the day; we obsess
about their health and welfare, where they are, and what they are doing;
we feel responsible for their success or failure; we run interference
between them and any other person or situation that may pose a threat
to them; it is our responsibility to make sure that their needs are met;
our day-to-day mood is attached to their day-to-day mood; we may feel
that without them, we will expire.

We *need* that person, we need them to be okay, and we need them
to love us. In at least some way, the object of our codependency defines
who we are. We may even experience a physical angst when we don't
know where they are, similar to withdrawal. Because the codependent
lives in a state of need, the codependent is constantly suffering in fear
of what may be happening with their object. A drug addict or an
alcoholic cannot function in his or her addiction without an enabling
codependent who will cover for them, lie for them, and put up with

them and whose denial is strong enough for the addict to lie his or her way out of responsibility. Addiction and codependency coexist.

The idea of codependency arose with Alcoholics Anonymous when it became clear that while an alcoholic develops a dependent relationship with alcohol, the spouse enters into an obsessive relationship with the alcoholic and thereby also with alcohol. The codependent's early attempts to control the alcoholic's drinking, such as demanding that he cease drinking, removing alcohol from the environment, and forbidding alcohol in the home, are ineffective. Any attempt to control the alcoholic's drinking without serious consequences to the alcoholic are fruitless.

The consequences of the alcoholic's drinking are linked closely to the codependent. The societal consequences of social rejection, loss of employment, and incarceration directly impact the family, and the codependent goes to great lengths to protect not only the alcoholic but the whole family from experiencing these consequences. The codependent wants to motivate the alcoholic to stop drinking but cannot bear the personal consequences, much less the consequences to the family. He or she lies to the employer, family members, and friends about the alcoholic's condition while complaining, then begging, threatening, nagging, and arguing with the alcoholic. The alcoholic is thus shielded from consequences and can use the spouse's behavior as an excuse to drink. The codependent's aversion to allowing the alcoholic and thus the family to experience painful consequences is the primary factor that *enables* the alcoholic to continue drinking.

The codependent, ineffective at trying to directly control the alcoholic, resorts to manipulation to try to stop the drinking. The codependent's efforts at "motivation" become increasingly bizarre, ranging from spying, planting electronic devices, attempts at physical restraint, outright lying about something that might scare the drinker, snooping through personal belongings, stalking, etc. The codependent feels trapped in the relationship and clings to the idea that he or she can make the alcoholic change. The addict gets his or her needs met by focusing on himself at the expense of others. The codependent gets his or her needs met by focusing on everyone else's needs at the expense of self. This is why the addict is so often the object of codependency. It is a perfect, completely crazy, and dysfunctional fit.

As codependents, we truly feel the other person's pain. We are compelled to alleviate their pain because it becomes our own, even if we are not invited to help. When we have a child or spouse or dear friend who has a problem, we find it completely irresponsible and selfish to sit by and watch them try to solve their problem. We might have the answers. We feel the responsibility. We believe that if we try hard enough, give enough of ourselves, we have the power to change the other person. We believe that if we matter enough to the alcoholic, he or she will stop drinking.

Although there are degrees of codependency in every kind of relationship, the parent-child relationship is set up from birth to develop codependency. It is well known that among most animals the mother is her fiercest when her baby is threatened. It is necessary for the survival of species.

We can hardly bear the thought that our child will have to experience the pain of rejection, failure, criticism, judgment, or even abuse. We know that he is a separate person, but the intensity of our love for him can lead us to feel his pain as our own. We cannot be happy when he is sad. We cannot be at peace when he is upset. Our culture reinforces this dynamic with the idea that "a mother is only as happy as her least happy child." We believe that we can take on the world, hoping to divert harshness and pain away from this awesome child.

We are the rescuers. We are their shields from harm. Hopefully, we can also be the ones who let go of the bicycle and watch him experience the delight of mastering a new skill. The child may skin a knee in the process, but the result is priceless. If we don't let go because we are too afraid of his pain, we rob the child of this joy, this new confidence. Our fear can disable this child.

Paradoxically, codependency encourages the very thing the parent is trying to avoid.

A dad who was so fearful that his daughter would fail her writing assignments repeatedly wrote or rewrote high school essays for her. She never learned to trust her ability and came to depend on her dad's help. This brilliant daughter was so paralyzed by writing assignments in college that she nearly dropped out. She was so fearful of her father's disappointment that she became suicidal. He not only robbed her of the opportunity to learn and grow in her ability to write, but he also stood in the way of her ability to trust her competence in all things.

A mom who wanted desperately for her son to feel good about himself and for him to love her repeatedly bought him apparel that she could not afford. She was willing to do without so that she could provide special things for him. He became entitled and arrogant, had no respect or gratitude for his mother, found her embarrassing because she didn't take care of herself or wear stylish clothes, and had no self-esteem.

This is the passive, enabling side of codependency. This type of codependent lives with resentment and self-pity because he or she presumes to know what everyone needs and does as much as is humanly possible for everyone, and yet no one appreciates it. As a passive codependent, our powerlessness is juxtaposed with our desire to control. We fail, try harder, and become disappointed, depressed victims.

There is another side of codependency: the aggressive, raging side. Those of us who are codependent may find ourselves raging at our child for not living up to our expectations. Our rage only masks a deep fear of powerlessness. We cannot tolerate the vulnerability we feel when our child is self-destructing, and we find strength in the power of rage. Our fear is expressed through anger as we try to "make" our child do what we know to be the right thing. Raging codependents take the drill-sergeant approach to their child's behavior problems.

A dad whose son would not get out of bed in the mornings tried throwing cold water on him and eventually dragging the mattress down the stairs, dumping his son out along the way. Every morning was a battle. The son took no responsibility for waking up. That became the dad's miserable chore. As soon as the dad was out of sight, the boy was back asleep. He was failing in school due to excessive absences, and the father was losing credibility at work for trailing in halfway through the morning each day. When the family started learning that the son's tardiness at school was not their responsibility, they allowed him to fail, and he did. His natural consequences were provided by the school, and he spent the summer in summer school. He was able to get himself out of bed without help before he went to college.

Our rage creates a wall of hostile resentment between us and our child. We become judgmental bullies.

The Cycle of Codependency.

When we try to shield our children from obstacles and protect them from their own mistakes, we become our own and their worst enemy. I was watching the children's calf scramble at the Houston Rodeo this year and found myself laughing at the irony of calves that would run like heck if the child was behind them but dig in and resist if the child was trying to pull them into the center of the arena. Would it be possible to rope a calf, hold the rope, get behind the calf, and chase him into the pen? It would be so much easier. As parents we have to quit trying to control the outcome and just get behind our children, watch them run in circles, and cheer when they finally get where they need to go.

Unless they are allowed to make mistakes, our children do not learn mastery over their lives and their self-esteem does not develop. Their dependency on us becomes hostile. We then react to their hostility and entitlement by feeling victimized and rejected, or by becoming judgmental and angry. We try to control them further by either trying to win their affection by doing even more for them, or by angrily threatening them and lashing out in judgment of their incompetence. This is the frustrating cycle of codependency.

They become more hostile. It continues until the codependent erupts in a rage.

Parents are incredibly susceptible to codependency. Parenting an infant requires that we put their needs ahead of our own. They begin life by literally being fused to the mother. They are physically separated at birth, but their survival requires our constant attention. Parenting a toddler requires the initiation of stronger boundaries with the child. With their increasing autonomy of thought and capability, the responsibilities for their lives are gradually transferred from the parent to the child, and the boundary separating the parent and child becomes more distinct. When do we let go of that bicycle and trust that our child will pedal? When we continue to do for the child all of those things that he or she could be doing for himself, we are undermining their development of tools needed to negotiate the world. By the time our child is adolescent, our boundaries have to be very strong, with a clear understanding of who is responsible for what.

The adolescent brain cannot make these distinctions. The adolescent will continue to function as he or she did at six or seven years old if that is allowed. The adolescent brain will opt for what is comfortable, easy, and the most fun. The codependent parent has difficulty trusting the child to take on a responsibility that has always been the parent's. The child will say, "That's your job. Why should I have to do it?" To which the codependent parent has no clear answer. The noncodependent parent will kindly say that she or he has rewritten the job description and just wants to make sure that everyone understands that from this day forward if they want clean clothes, they will have to wash them. Then, we may have to watch our child wearing dirty clothes for a while.

It is awesome to watch a toddler. He has no self-consciousness. He has no shame. He is comfortable within his own experience. It is beautiful. Those precious qualities will not persevere into adulthood. Somewhere between those sweet, innocent early years and adolescence, as the world becomes bigger, as expectations are felt, as social experiences become increasingly complex, self-consciousness appears. The debris of growing up. What we don't embrace is that this debris is the stuff that gives him opportunities to build skills and also nurture his confidence and esteem. He or she *needs* this stuff. We, as parents, can recognize the experience as painful and love them through it, but the moment we try to rescue them out of it or control them through it, we have blown the chance for our child to grow emotionally.

The child of a codependent becomes incapable of negotiating the realities of normal disappointment and failure. Akin to entitlement, children of codependents blame all of their problems on us, because we have established that we are supposed to make everything right. This child has no self-esteem because he has no idea how to work through mistakes, overcome failures, or work hard to reach goals. This child feels no gratitude, and we are hurt. This child knows that we are easily hurt and figures out how to play us.

Addiction cannot survive without at least one playable person who can be manipulated. In the case of the addicted teen, both parents are targets. We start with our assumptions, mental habits of parenting, and pump up the volume. One parent increases attempts to control, fearing that the nurturing parent is making things easy for the teen, and thus becomes ineffective as a parent. The other increases the caretaking, fearing that the controlling parent is damaging the teen's self-esteem and creating an unsafe home, and thus becomes ineffective as a parent. They undermine each other. Once the addict figures out how to play one parent against the other, the addiction has found the perfect petri dish in which to flourish, and the marriage is threatened.

Rethink Parenting

As long as we function on autopilot, our parenting is a reaction to our experience of being parented. We are either doing things the way our parents did them, or we are trying to parent in opposition to our experience of our parents. Either way, we are reacting to our own parents, based upon our experiences, in the environment in which we grew up, and are not necessarily parenting in response to our child's needs. The goal is to become intentional, to examine our many choices and respond to each situation, and to use this conscious intent and knowledge to override those knee-jerk reactions that developed as habits during our childhood.

The first thought of most parents who discover their child's drug use is to control the child by moving, grounding him, restricting his contact with others, etc. We create a prison for ourselves trying to confine our child, which is impossible. Codependent parents do not want our children to experience hard consequences like jail or getting kicked out of school. We run interference, blame the other kids, make excuses, and are furious with our child because he or she is ungrateful and keeps up the bad behavior. But those consequences are absolutely necessary. Our child has lessons to learn and will get the opportunity to learn them through challenging, sometimes painful experiences, either now or as an adult. When we step in to rescue the child or try to control or prevent the experience, we rob our child of the opportunity to grow through the normal experiences in life and the challenges will get even harder.

Short-Term Pain for Long-Term Gain

The beauty of having to correct mistakes, overcome failure, and feel painful consequences of our irresponsible actions is that we learn. If we fail to learn from them, the mistakes, failures, and irresponsible actions will repeat. The older we get, the harsher the consequences. If a child never learns to respect gravity because we couldn't let go of the bicycle, there are horrendous accidents looming ahead. Ultimately, gravity is going to be learned. It's a little painful for the child who falls down but saves a lot of hurt later in life.

While the codependent uses a myriad of tactics, here are the most prominent that I see.

Denial

Codependents lack self-honesty. Codependents have the ability to see our world as we wish to see it, as we believe it should be. In order to grow out of codependency we must face our *denial* and be willing to see reality. Denial has kept us in a bubble of safety and happiness, or so we pretend. Others can see what we refuse to see. When faced with the serious problem of teen drug use, we just don't want to see it. A codependent can live with an alcoholic who is drinking for a long time, living in denial, perplexed at his strange behavior, but trusting his words instead of our own observations.

Avoidance

Codependents like to be comfortable. We avoid our personal problems by focusing on "smokescreen" issues that take up space in our thinking, like what our spouse is doing wrong, what our coworkers are saying, politics, gossip, resentment, injustice, and all of the things that are wrong with whoever suggests that we change. We become perfectionistic workaholics, volunteer for everything that comes in front of us, and overload our calendars to avoid looking at ourselves. We fall in love or become engaged in hobbies and projects and commitments that isolate us from the realities of life. This is the way that we shy from our fear and feel productive. We create all of this so that we can stay comfortable and not face our fears. It is very common for new parents in an APG to get focused on what is wrong with the organization and how they need to fix it. This is just a way to avoid their pain and feel of value in the face of their powerlessness and feared personal incompetency.

Compliance

Codependents often go along with what others say or want, regardless of their conflicting feelings, beliefs, or instincts. This kind of *compliance* often leads us to resent the people with whom we comply, but we do it nevertheless, to avoid conflict or just because we are exhausted. We like reasons and excuses. Ask us a simple yes or no question and we will tell you a story about why. Compliance includes rescuing and protecting another person from the consequences he or she has earned by virtue of his or her choices. We will go along with others' wrong thinking and justifications. A codependent woman complained that her husband repeatedly asked as they were driving out of the driveway, "Where would you like to go for dinner?" and after she answered, he would say, "Well, I was thinking I want to go to ABC Restaurant [not her suggestion]," and he would drive there. He always asked the question and then disregarded her answer and drove to the restaurant he wanted. Her therapist suggested that she change her response to, "I would like to go to XYZ, and in fact I think I will head on over there. Would you care to join me? If not, I will need to take my car."

Control

Codependents are all about *control*. We control others by doing their work, by not letting them grow, by keeping them dependent, by not holding them accountable, by avoiding the hard conversations, by making excuses for them and covering their mistakes, by not trusting them to develop competency on their own, and by emotionally manipulating them into doing things the way we want them done and eventually make them dependent enough on us that they cannot leave us.

Codependency is heavy and makes relationships feel burdensome. Codependents believe that they have the power and responsibility to fix other people, to change them. Codependents experience confusion between control and love, stemming from childhood boundary dysfunction in their family of origin.

In healthy relationships, people share responsibilities and do things for each other willingly. This is how relationships work. If a pattern of inequality develops, if things are done begrudgingly to avoid a fight or to avoid feeling selfish, if things are done out of fear of being rejected or of being criticized, if it feels like an obligation, and if it is not something that we do out of genuine interest in sharing the activity with the other, the behavior is codependent.

Chapter 9

UNITED FRONT

....

If you do not change direction,
you may end up where you are heading.
—Lao Tzu

....

Most marriages begin in a ceremony that symbolically unites the two into one unit. Maintaining the unity in the marriage doesn't require that anyone sacrifice their uniqueness, but rather it means that each respects the other and is willing to work through compromises. It means that the other person's wellbeing is considered in all decisions and actions. This process requires a fairly constant commitment to the concept of unity and often gets disregarded as couples establish a practical separation of responsibilities and duties, which is necessary to manage a household while raising children. Each person trusts that the other will make decisions that are in the best interest of the family. Instead of discussing every decision, it becomes easier to just do what we want to do and not consult our partner. In many marriages this works quite well, with both partners respecting each other's opinions and keeping the focus on the best choices for each other and the family.

The drift away from unity starts with our decision to avoid some of those discussions because we know there will be disagreement. We feel that our way is Right, which means their way is Wrong. If one partner will not compromise, there is nothing to gain from a conversation that will lead to a huge fight or to the less stubborn backing down. We start to think of the other partner as our competition. We may start to exaggerate or withhold information in order to get our way because we believe that we are Right. The marriage becomes a sort of game, and information is used to our advantage. This dynamic often reveals basic distrust or disrespect between the partners.

In a functional family, the parents are in communication with each other, cooperating and compromising to maintain a unit of authority over their household and fostering respect from the children. With this united front, the child can trust that the message will be consistent and that they will not be able to get away with unhealthy behavior. Each of the children has relationships with each other and with both parents.

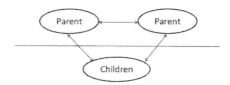

Appropriate parent-child boundaries

When our child is miserable, failing in some way, in some kind of danger, we begin to look for reasons and ways to rescue him or her. We may carry a nagging fear that it is our fault. We try harder. We see the other parent become more punitive and strict. We offset that by being more lenient and understanding. Or we see the "nurturing" parent going easy on the child's obviously wrong behavior and feel that we need to step up the intensity of harsh punishments. As these efforts are ineffective, the child gets worse and the parents become extremely polarized.

We deflect our pain and shame by magnifying the "errors" of the other parent. We are powerless. We are victims of the bullying parent or victims of the enabling parent. Resentment sets in. The punishing parent fulfills the role by becoming a bully. He or she is now the enemy. The nurturing parent becomes the child's ally in desperate attempts to offset the harshness of the bully, becoming the enabler. Each parent pumps up the volume on ineffective patterns, desperately trying to neutralize the damage being done by the other parent. No matter what the child does, both parents are completely ineffective because each undermines the other. Neither parent sees a way to stop reacting because they are unable to see that each is creating as much craziness as the other. The child has successfully created the triangulation needed to get away with using drugs.

Addiction, like a nasty virus, feeds on the weaknesses in not just the user, but all of his or her relationships, choosing the weakest point to infect. Weaknesses in the parents' relationship are particularly vulnerable to attack. Parents whose teen is addicted to alcohol or drugs are each carrying such a heavy load of emotional turmoil that they need to share the burden, to lean on each other. If they do not trust each other, neither has the energy to give that desperately needed support to the other and the marriage begins to fail.

Deterioration of family boundaries as child triangulates parents

When the child holds the power in the family, all of the relationships suffer and the family becomes dysfunctional. The parent-child boundary is lost, and the parents' relationship is damaged. The child's relationship with both parents deteriorates. Siblings get lost.

With this boundary confusion, both parents become hyper-focused on feelings of betrayal by the other parent, and the drug-abusing child runs the house. The child becomes the hockey puck that is used by each parent to attempt to score against the other parent. The child plays along, learning how to masterfully manipulate the parents in the process.

Many families come for help on the brink of divorce or recently divorced. Divorce will not solve this problem and in fact makes it worse for everyone. Divorced parents have little motivation to get along with each other. The children can easily manipulate either parent and can lie about the other parent's decisions or behavior and be believed. For the teen to begin to take stock of his or her life, *the parents have to unify in their approach to parenting.* When the relationship has dissolved, this is very difficult. Sometimes the harsher parent is abandoned by the children and the nurturing parent is overwhelmed and forced to become a disciplinarian. Sometimes one parent can develop a strong presence for the children without the other parent, as long as the undermining has stopped. This is better but remains tragic. Children suffer greatly the loss of a parent, no matter how dysfunctional he or she is.

It reminds me of a trust exercise I observed on a river in which two people held the opposite ends of a rope and leaned back as far as they could over the rim of a boat. If either let go, they would both fall into the water. They had to figure out how to cooperate and trust each other in order to get back into the boat. Of course the solution is for both to move to the center, but it is tricky and takes a lot of strength and cooperation.

Oddly, if one parent quits playing the game, the other usually changes roles. When the enabler stops enabling, the bully surprisingly becomes softer and worries about the child. When the bully backs off and becomes more loving, the enabler is likely to pick up some slack and begin to impose discipline.

The addiction cannot survive without an enabler. When parents are united, they interrupt each other's urge to either rescue or bully the child. When the child has triangulated the parents as described above, the process of repairing the dysfunction is not easy but is absolutely necessary to protect all of the children. The parents have to set aside their egos, stop blaming, and choose a new direction. They have to cooperate, compromise, and once again work together in unison. The boundaries in the family have to become clear and healthy.

This is a simple concept but incredibly hard to accomplish. If you like to fight, then don't kid yourself and blame your spouse. Some people just love a good fight. Sometimes anger is an easier, more powerful feeling than fear or shame, but there is always some sort of pain or fear behind the anger. There is nothing wrong with being angry. However, acting out of anger against your spouse or child is dangerous. No one can unite with a person who wants to fight and has to be right.

If you want to develop a united front, you must both agree that what you are doing is miserable and not working. If you can agree on that point, you can change the direction of your parenting:

1. Trade roles. The enabling parent must become the disciplinarian, and the bully must become nurturing. This is powerful.

2. Agree on rules and their associated consequences in a time of relative peace when the two of you can think clearly. See the "Rules and Consequences" chapter. Never threaten a consequence that you are not going to enforce. This is dishonest and manipulative.

3. When talking to your children, use "we" terms. Mom, say, "Your dad and I have made this decision …" Dad, say, "Your mom and I have talked this over, and we feel …" When you aren't sure what to do in a situation, or when you are being pressed for an answer to a request, say, "I will need to take a little time and discuss this with your mother before I give you an answer, so if you must have an answer right at this minute, I have to say no." This is unity in parenting.

4. Enforce all consequences. Never allow excuses, promises of better behavior in the future, or the child's criticism of the other parent or your stupid rules to interfere with your commitment to parent your children in unison with your partner.

5. Understand how hard this is for your coparent. Be understanding but strong when your spouse has a weak moment or tries to justify undermining the unity. If one of you continually undermines the other after this process, seek strong support from a parenting group or an Al-Anon group and sponsors.

Invariably, what happens as this is played out is that both parents gravitate toward the middle. The enabler becomes more resolved and can stand up to the child. The bully becomes more nurturing and empathic, now trusting that his partner will no longer undermine his authority.

Chapter 10

RULES AND CONSEQUENCES

....

Life is a succession of lessons which must be
lived to be understood.
—Emerson

....

Parenting without consistent rules and consequences really does not work well. Most of us have rules in our heads and expect our children to live by them, or we have a lot of rules that we lay out for our kids and do not effectively enforce them. What I mean by "effectively" enforcing rules is that we need to consistently, strategically, and lovingly enforce consequences as part of a plan of which the kids are well aware.

Most of us don't create a plan for consequences of rule violations.

As humans develop, our anticipation of negative consequences informs our decisions. As a society, we use laws and associated punishments to deter crime. If a law is not enforced, it is useless. Individually, as we mature we internalize laws of morality that preclude stealing, harming others, etc. Adolescents are not there yet.

Adolescents want to be treated like adults. They are indignant when you don't treat them like adults, but they are not adults. Ironically they are happiest when we reduce the ambiguity in their lives, when they have clear rules that they know will be enforced without fail. They need years to develop their internal set of controls over their behavior while we are in charge. We must help them develop positive habits of living. They cannot do it without help.

We feel our powerlessness and have little hope that we can regain our personal strength.

It's okay. Now is the time to take a new approach. If you haven't already been brought to your knees by your teen's behavior, you can avoid it! If you have already been there, it is not too late. Form a united front with your co-parent. Create rules and consequences. Do not wait for a "good" time to do this. Just give yourself time to calm down, breathe, consult someone you trust, pray, meditate, or whatever you do personally to quiet your mind so that you can access your wisdom.

Always respond. Never react. Reactions are emotional and personal ... just buttons formed of our emotional memories being pushed. Responses are thoughtful and rational. The goal of rules and consequences is to set firm boundaries around acceptable behavior in our home so that it is safe for everyone. Once the rules are established and the consequences are determined, there is no need to panic. There is nothing to fight over. Our child knew the rule and knew the consequence. By breaking the rule, he or she chose to receive the consequence. It's not a punishment that you are imposing. It is the child's informed choice.

Consequences must be enforced with love and compassion. Our children are trying to grow through adolescence, and in many cases it is a living hell. By teaching them how to live within rules, we hope to save them from having to experience this process as an adult, when the societal consequences are huge.

In order to facilitate change, unwanted behaviors must be targeted and consequences must be strategically selected, paired, and carried out in a loving, caring, empathic way.

The beauty of this process is that once implemented, the responsibility for the consequence is in the hands of the rule-breaker. The next time the child repeats the behavior, you don't need to argue or discuss anything. The rules and consequences are clearly decided. Your plan is in place, and your child knows that his or her choices will lead to some specific known outcome.

We empower him to make self-protective choices. We respect his right to take ownership of his decisions, and therefore he cannot blame us or anyone else for his misery. There is nothing to argue about, and you can be very warm and empathic. "I am so sorry to see that you have made this decision, but my job is to follow through on my commitment to honor my word, so …"

The Shots

Our laws have become so complicated and the legal system so confusing that "right" and "wrong" are often overridden by crafty legal maneuvering. Liken this to an intelligent and persuasive, smooth-talking teenager. They can talk their way out of almost anything and sound reasonable. Parents fall for it. They begin to doubt their own reality. "Maybe that really was oregano in the baggie," or "Maybe he really was just holding the drugs for a friend." Simplify the rules, and do not accept excuses.

Your rules need to target the behavior you are concerned about. Trust your instinct. Be direct and concise. If you make it complicated, you are doomed. This is not a legal document. You have the final word and will be the deciding factor in the event of any gray area. The rules are always subject to change should you find it necessary.

Choose your rules carefully, in unison with your coparent. You do not need more than five or six rules. The idea of six rules came from the concept of a six-shooter, the old revolving barrel pistol. You get six shots, so you need to choose carefully (Meehan, 1996). The shots must be strategically aimed at behavior that is unhealthy for your family. Dishonesty, disrespect for another or oneself, illegal acts, breaking commitments, and entitlement are some that are typically targeted, but you may have others.

Do not waste a shot on things that make you happy but really just feed your need to control, like keeping his or her room clean and taking out the garbage. This confuses "chores" with serious life choices worthy of a shot. If he or she is being respectful and following commitments, those other things will eventually fall into place.

Examples of shots used by families in recovery:

- Work a recovery program to the satisfaction of your counselor (meaning, stay engaged and actively participating in a twelve-step program and seeing a counselor).
- Do not engage in dishonesty of any kind by omission or commission.
- Treat all family members (including self) and their property with respect.
- Each family member must be productively engaged in work, school, or a combination of the two.

I want to reiterate that our children mimic our behavior. We are the models. If we aren't living by the same rules that we expect our child to live by, how can we expect the child to buy in to this process? If we hold our children to a higher standard than we are willing to live by, we are being hypocritical and our kids absolutely know it. We may have to bring our behavior up to par before this process can go smoothly.

For most of us, particularly as we begin this process, it is difficult to determine where to draw the line in the sand. Wherever we draw it, our child is likely to step over it. If we do not want them to use drugs or alcohol illegally, then make it clear. They will test the limit. If you tell them that a little recreational use is okay with you, then be ready to deal with the likelihood that your child will take it one step further.

The Consequences

There are three essential components to an effective consequence. It has to be strategic, be motivating, and offer a path to redemption. The development of consequences takes a little out-of-the-box thinking.

Strategic consequences are designed around the natural adult consequence of an infraction. They should be a "softer" consequence than would be experienced in adulthood. It is not strategic to require a child who lies to you to mow the lawn. It is strategic to require a child who has been dishonest to give up privileges that require trust.

If our child does break a rule and we don't have a plan, our first impulse is to have a serious talk with them and/or to ground them. There is a time for a serious talk and a time for grounding, but not as a knee-jerk reaction.

A serious talk. We talk to them about it. We plan our perfect presentation of the situation as we see it, expecting the wisdom and logic that we present to serve as a deterrent to future infractions. In an effort to cope with the situation, our brains resist the reality that our teens, even though they love us, do not really believe that we know what we are talking about (even if we are experts). Further, even if they are genuinely repentant and promise with every intent to never repeat this infraction, when that limbic system is in charge and the moment is no longer driven by logic, a consequence that involves having a discussion with a parent is not particularly deterring.

Sometimes this serious talk involves yelling, name-calling, or threatening or may deteriorate into violence. We cannot hear what people say when they are yelling. As soon as the yelling starts, the listening stops. Not only is yelling ineffective, but it also further damages the relationship, your own self-esteem, and your child's trust in you. It is also abusive and may have consequences for you. If you are abusive or bullying, your child will be abusive and a bully.

The time for the serious talk is *before* the rule is broken. If you have not talked seriously with your children about the rules of your home, rules that are designed to protect them and serve as guidelines for their development, the time to do it is *not* when you are upset and your child is fearful.

Grounding. We may believe we can keep them from having another opportunity to repeat their mistake by keeping them within our eyesight. Most grounding has the intent to remove the child from social contact. Of course this means that we are also grounded. Eventually, we go to work or a movie or sleep, and they have the opportunity to break out. If they don't and are physically cut off from their peers, they have an abundance of ways to connect virtually, and their skills are generally much better than ours at managing social media. If we take their phone, they can use a computer to do everything the phone does. If we take the computer, tablet, and phone, they use another computer. If we also remove our own and any sibling devices, the whole family is grounded and cut off, and it becomes a huge power struggle between parents and teens—one we typically will lose. Usually we get exhausted and either retract the punishment or start making exceptions fairly quickly.

One father told me that his son absolutely would not relapse when discharged from a residential substance abuse treatment program because he "would not allow it." The boy overdosed in his room with both parents sleeping down the hall. We cannot control the behavior of others. We have to guide our children, but as soon as we get into trying to control them, we lose the leverage of the family relationships and any trust they may have had in us.

Grounding is similar to adult imprisonment. It is a punishment that may make the outside world safer but does not in itself rehabilitate or remediate the offender's tendency to break a law. Recidivism among our prison population is clear evidence that this is not an effective tool to use with our children.

Another risk of grounding is that our teens become depressed when isolated.

The time to establish any form of grounding as a potential consequence is before the rule is broken. It is totally reasonable to remove driving privileges if a teen sneaks the car out, lies about where he or she is going, gets a traffic ticket, has a wreck, or drinks. A person who drives needs to be trustworthy. This protects not only the teen but all of the rest of the drivers. It makes sense to take away a cell phone if a teen has sent or even taken an explicit "selfie." This teen probably needs some therapy and an old flip-phone with no texting or photo ability, which means it needs to be a very limited device (you can search the Internet for the best cell phones for kids or a wrist phone without camera). Tell your child when you provide his or her very first phone that you will be monitoring his or her use. Explain what is not acceptable and why.

Consequences are not the same as punishment. Punishment typically inflicts misery without creating a solution. The ultimate consequence for dangerous or destructive behavior, including drug or alcohol abuse, is to be moved out of the home in order to both remediate the problem and to protect the rest of the family. This is powerful. This is complicated and painful, but you cannot allow a child to inflict violence upon others or self-destruct with drugs and alcohol. If you do, your child will end up in prison or deceased. Call the police if necessary.

Removal from the home is the equivalent of banishment from the tribe. In an Alternative Peer Group program, seasoned parents often volunteer their homes as a temporary host homes for children who have made a choice that requires that they move out of their home. The host home must be carefully vetted, be well known to the family, have a track record of strong recovery and loving accountability to rules in their home, and have healthy, sober, same-sex children in the home. Some cities have shelters for adolescents. When these are not an option, we sometimes have found family members who are capable and willing hosts. This is disruptive for both families. The child should not take any comfort items to the host home, only several changes of clothes.

You cannot legally kick your child out of your house. You can provide alternative housing, though, that creates the same effect. Residential rehabilitation treatment centers may be a good choice. Remember, punishment does not work. Parenting in anger does not work. Your attitude is very important.

I never recommend grounding as a consequence for an adolescent. I often recommend alternative social activities. Isolation and loneliness are dangerous for children and adolescents who are having behavior problems. They are filled with self-loathing, fear of their own inadequacy, and mistrust of their parents. Suicide is too often seen as a reasonable alternative. Adolescents do not have any concept of a short-term problem. Every misery feels like it will last forever.

How to Develop Shots and Consequences

We have to be consistent, committed, united, and loving as we go through this process. Work together to create the rules. If the list is complicated, start over or delete the detail. They have to be simple. This is not a list that is meant to determine every aspect of every family member's life. This is not a legally binding contract. You don't need definitions. You know when you are disrespected. They know when they feel disrespected. If you know someone who has been through this, you might ask for their feedback. If you have a twelve-step sponsor, review the list with him or her.

Once satisfied, show them to your children. Surprisingly, children often receive this well. Or if your child throws the list at you or otherwise fails to participate in the conversation, you are doing exactly what is needed. At this point kids don't believe we will actually follow through with any of this, having tried threatening or scare tactics in the past. This is different. This is what you *will* do. Without fail. He or she will call your bluff.

Therefore, do not list a rule for behavior that is not critical. Do not list a consequence that you are unwilling to carry out. These rules will be tested. If a rule is repeatedly violated in spite of the applied consequence, the consequence is not sufficiently motivating. One teen told me that he was required to pay restitution for anything that he took or broke in the house. That's it. By the time he was seventeen, he owed his parents a huge sum of money and had no intent to pay it back.

Post the rules somewhere visible, possibly on the refrigerator. They are always subject to revision, so if they aren't perfect, just start with something that you *will* do, even if it is just taking cable TV out of the child's room if you catch him smoking weed. It won't remedy the behavior, but if you follow through, you will gain confidence that you can take action that is more strategic and motivating and revise the consequence.

Enforcing the Rules

At first your child will not believe that you will carry out a consequence. When you do, he or she will want to discuss or negotiate it. Do not get drawn into this tactic. Your child is not listening to your explanation with an interest in understanding your decision; he or she is listening for a loophole so he or she can argue, push your buttons, and play on your desire for him or her to agree with your decision. We seem to believe that, in the middle of a long argument, the other person will say, "Oh, now that you have explained yourself so clearly, I understand and agree with your point of view." Has this *ever* happened? If you disagree, an argument will absolutely be a waste of time. This is a parent who wants to be seen as reasonable and empathic. Those are great things to want, but it is not reasonable to allow a teen to self-destruct and it certainly isn't empathic to know that your child is incapable of self-correcting and nevertheless refuse to take on that role for him.

Talking is not effective or motivating to change your child's behavior and is a delay tactic on the part of your teen. Action with compassion is extremely effective.

Never allow a promise of future behavior to dissuade you from taking action on today's problem. The first time your child breaks a shot, he or she will promise to never do this thing again if you just won't enforce any consequence. If you buy into this, you are just delaying your own discomfort and giving the teen one more opportunity to act out.

If you establish a rule but do not follow through on the consequence, not only is the rule useless, but you have lied to your child and he cannot trust you to honor a commitment. If we do not carry out consequences, we are parenting out of fear. If you back down and offer a second or third chance, you are basically letting your child know that it's okay to repeat the behavior one or two more times. This is just fear on your part. This is you, hoping that you never have to actually impose a consequence. They will do it until they have a consequence that gets their attention.

When you back down, you are yielding your power, proving that your word doesn't mean anything and that you are powerless. No child or adolescent wants a powerless parent. It makes them furious and insecure. This breeds disrespect.

Some kids facing consequences run away and hit the streets. They hope this will teach the parents to not mess with them. This is terrifying. If he runs away, call the police and report him as a runaway. If you know where he is, tell the police. If a friend is harboring him, call the other parent and discuss the problem. Harboring a runaway is a serious offense.

Do not rescue your child by promising to back off the rules. You are in a standoff. If you cave in to alleviate your fear, you will never be trusted again. He is uncomfortable. This will be incredibly miserable for you, but you are powerless. I have never known a teen to stay out permanently. They usually return within a few days, but those days are among the hardest of your life. You are staking your claim, making your personal commitment as a parent to protect your home and to love your child enough to not tolerate behavior that is beneath his dignity, destructive, and undermines his self-worth.

If your child threatens suicide, get him directly to a psychiatric hospital. If he won't go, call the police, who will immediately escort him there. Even if he is bluffing, he needs to know that you take that threat seriously. You can be making one of two possible mistakes: not taking him when you should have, or taking him when he doesn't need it. One leads to death and the other to a long and boring night in a hospital waiting room and hours being evaluated. He will know that you are a person of your word, that you will take him seriously, and that you will go to great lengths to keep him safe. If the behavior was attention-seeking, he will most likely not want to do that again.

Teens want everything *now*, and when an unanticipated situation calls for a consequence, they want an immediate decision from us. Often, we back off simply because of the energy it takes. In order to respond strategically, you can say instead, "I can promise you that I will give you an answer but not until I am ready, and I cannot tell you exactly when that will be."

Of course, this is very anxiety-provoking for the teen. This gives the teen some time to anticipate and rethink the situation. If you are still worrying about rescuing your child from anxiety, this will be hard for you. Let him or her sit with that anxiety for a while. It may take an hour, or it may take a day. Parents need to work together to establish a consequence, setting aside personal differences and old resentments. This may be difficult and is addressed in the United Front chapter.

Consult others who may have faced this problem before. Read. Talk to professionals.

If you do the work to become aware of your choices, and if you choose to stay out of drama and fear, you will be able to respond to the changing needs of your family and your life, rather than reacting ineffectively with a chaotic explosion of emotion.

Chapter 11

FEAR AND LOVE

....

The greatest obstacles to inner peace are disturbing
emotions such as anger, attachment, fear and suspicion,
while love and compassion and a sense of universal
responsibility are the sources of peace and happiness.

If you have fear of some pain or suffering, you should
examine whether there is anything you can do about it. If
you can, there is no need to worry about it; if you cannot
do anything, then there is also no need to worry.
—Dalai Lama

....

When we live in fear of pain, try to anticipate and avoid the pain, try
to rescue our loved ones from pain, we spend our lives living on the
dark side—preoccupied with worry, judgment, perfectionism—trying
to avoid the unavoidable.

When we live our lives according to basic principles I have tried to
explain in this book, life gets really simple, calm, and easy. It's not that
there are no more problems. There are just no "Oh my God!" moments
of panic.

Something beautiful happens when we quit trying to make other
people be who we think they should be or who we want them to be.

When we no longer allow our hopes and dreams to hinge on the actions of others, we can either accept our reality or change it. My life today is the current state of my path, totally and completely the result of every decision and action I have taken in the past. I can change my present, and I can change my future. I cannot change anything that happened in the past. I do not need to limit my future based upon past events. I can come to embrace my failures as the minor, and sometimes major, explosions in the laboratory of life. Every day that I live on a new path becomes a beautiful memory in my past with the next sunrise.

The APG program in which I work has a leadership course available to young adults (eighteen to twenty-one) who have completed their early recovery work and desire a substantial new challenge. I had the incredible fortune to have been invited to join this group on a rafting trip down the Colorado River through the Grand Canyon several years ago. I was to meet the group at the bottom of the South Kaibob trail on the riverbank near Phantom Ranch. They would have been on the river for a week and would arrive at this point around the time that I should finish my descent from the rim. I sent my gear ahead, traveled to Arizona, drove to the canyon, parked the car, filled my hydration pack (which instantly froze), and stepped over the edge of the canyon at 5:00 a.m. alone in the dark in seventeen degrees of cold for the seven-mile hike down the steep slope to the river. I wasn't sure how long it would take me to make the hike. I wasn't sure how we would end up coordinating our arrival at the beach or what I would do if they weren't there. I didn't know any of the group members well, was more than forty years older than all but a few of them, twenty-five years older than the oldest guide, and was taking the spot of a man who they all knew and dearly loved. This man had offered to give me his spot for the last two weeks of the trip. He would hike out when I hiked in.

I had fear. I was alone. I am so uncool that surely I would be odd to this group. I would be off the grid for two weeks. I didn't fear the physical rigor or the rafting or the rapids.

I just knew that the trail led to the river and the river only flows in one direction, so I just went. I was in good shape at sixty-three years old but underestimated my knees, which were in excruciating pain after four miles downhill. The last three miles were slow, and every step so painful that I took anti-inflammatory medication and stopped frequently. A passerby stopped and said a prayer for my knees. About a half-mile from the bottom I could see them relaxing on the river beach. I wanted to just roll down the rest of the way! I wondered if it would be possible to create a sled out of my pack and slide down, but the rocks and cacti weren't too inviting. I continued on slowly, and upon my arrival one of the young men gave me a hug, which nearly knocked me over my unstable legs. It was sunny and beautiful, the group was incredibly welcoming, and my fear had been completely unwarranted. I had never thought to fear the pain in my knees.

I took *Dancing with Life* by Phillip Moffitt and spent two weeks off the grid. I learned some new things and became reintroduced to old thoughts presented in a new way. It's okay to be exactly who I am, where I am. It is my reality. To need anything more simply sets me up for the suffering of not being or having what I have created the illusion that I need.

There are two primary emotions: fear and love. I sometimes think of it as the dark and the light. Label the two polar opposites as you like. One encompasses all that is good and the other, all that is unpleasant or even horrid. I heard one woman describe it as either walking toward or away from God.

All negative, destructive emotions come from the dark. Anger, resentment, jealousy, pettiness, criticism, judgment, perfectionism, self-righteousness, guilt, shame, and worry all emerge from our thought processes, our unrealistic expectations, our self-focus, our forgetting that we can choose. Fear is fundamental to all dark feelings. Fear is the emotional result of clinging desperately to a need or a perceived need. The fear that we feel if faced with danger comes from fear of injury, pain, or death. The fear that underlies all of those nasty, unpleasant emotions is psychological, based in a perceived need for things, people, and ego-inflating conditions. The "dark side" of emotions is fertile ground for the ego to get out of control.

I need …

- recognition, or
- to be loved, or
- to be heard, or
- to be noticed, or
- to buy that dress, or
- to live in that house, or
- to be with that man, or
- to own that jewelry.

I need my children to …

- be happy,
- be confident,
- avoid risks,
- escape pain,
- be successful,
- love me, and
- appreciate me.

As soon as we need something, we place the power to satisfy our need outside of our being. We forfeit the ability to self-guide and self-correct our lives. We end up feeling jealous, angry, judgmental, critical, ashamed, insulted, petty, anxious, and afraid.

I recently read a quote about strong women that made me smile: "The funny thing about a strong woman is that she doesn't need you … she wants you. And, if you start slacking she'll be content without you" (unknown author).

The "not needing" allows us to love purely, unencumbered with expectations and requirements. I worked with a couple whose relationship deteriorated when the wife found her voice and tried to establish autonomy. The husband became very critical and controlling. She had a hard time feeling love for him when he acted as if he was entitled to her. He was convinced that he "needed" her love. Needing a partner who is responsible for completing us or for keeping us happy is just asking too much. He was so angry with her for refusing to take on that role that he called her names, threatened to divorce her, and was continually sullen in her presence. This wasn't making him more appealing or loveable to his wife. He had to learn how to fill up his heart. She could not fill the hole left in his heart by his miserable childhood. He had to release her from that role and become the man he wanted to be. Then he could love himself enough to really love her.

Each of us has to figure out what our fear is about, but fearing the judgment of self and others is about living in our shame. In my teens and into my twenties I used to fear that if anyone really knew the truth about me they would certainly have nothing to do with me. I needed acceptance. I became whatever I thought you wanted me to be, just to be liked, and I didn't even realize I was doing it. Adolescents are overwhelmed with this fear. What if I don't fit in? They need their world to reflect that they are okay because on the inside they are not sure.

Fear is normal, and we all have it. Feeling fear is informative. Acting out of fear in relationships will drive you to destruction. Fear and outcome are reciprocal. Fear causes the very thing that is feared to become reality.

People die every day because of the power of fear. Wars are fought because one group fears another. Road rage is fear acted upon. One careless or rude driver can easily create fear in another. Sometimes the fear is real and you nearly crashed … "Whew! That was close!" after which you calm down. This is normal. However, when our egos get involved, we might begin to rant. "How dare that guy cut me off like that? Who does he think he is? I'll show him who's who!" (A reminder of our own feared insignificance and impermanence.) The road rage is more likely to get us killed than the event that started the whole thing—being cut off.

Jealousy destroys relationships by creating insanity in one or both persons based upon a fear of rejection or abandonment. Jealousy causes abandonment by acting out the fear of abandonment. Jealousy insults the integrity of your partner. People don't cheat because they don't love you; they cheat because they don't love themselves. Your partner's integrity in the relationship isn't out of love for you; it is because he is a person of integrity who loves himself and does not want to be a person who cheats. If your partner cheats, you can decide to accept or reject the relationship. You can't change him or her. You can't change the past.

The more we fear our own imperfections, the worse our perfectionism and criticism and judgment of others becomes, and this attitude is likely to push others away. We have been taught that we should not have imperfections and thus have been set up to feel shame because we *do* have imperfections. Furthermore, people don't really like others who appear to be perfect or pretend to be perfect. They are not trustworthy because they are hiding their true selves from us. It is when we are honest and open, humble about our imperfections, learn not to take ourselves so seriously, that we become lovable to others.

What does it mean when we are critical of others? It means that we have given someone else the power to establish our worth and they have failed.

We want to feel that we are good enough to coexist with the rest of our tribe ... that we belong. When some of us don't feel that sense of belonging, we lie to ourselves that we actually are superior and enjoy the privilege of judgment. We think that we know something. We think that we are right. That smugness is fear-based and is manifest in efforts to control the people in our world, and to avoid the shame of our imperfection. The world may feel safe if we are right, if those who disagree are wrong, because then we can exactly control or predict the next thing that will happen in our lives. We cling to that belief because not knowing is very scary to many of us.

Others who don't feel secure in their sense of belonging—in a relationship or a group—seek constant reassurance. The incessant need to be reassured by others can actually become annoying and drive others away. The fear of being left actually leads to being left.

Criticism is never constructive. It is destructive, an excuse to stand in judgment, inflict pain or shame, and feel righteous. When I was in fourth grade, my girlfriends and I used to say, "I don't mean to be mean, but ..." followed by some harsh criticism about something completely trivial. My mother heard me say that once and cut me off by saying, "Then don't say it." That was the last time I used that phrase. She was right. I didn't want to be mean, but I did mean to be critical,

Thank you for choosing us
for your meal
today!

Server: Tristan M
Check #21   Table 56
Ordered: 06/09/20 5:17 PM

Input Type
           C (EMV Chip Read)
VISA CREDIT   xxxxxxxx8255
Time   5:59 PM

Transaction Type   Sale
Authorization   Approved
Approval Code   05641D
Payment ID   XcWmnkTsTfdX
Application ID
                A0000000031010
Application Label
                   VISA CREDIT
Terminal ID
Card Reader

           MAGTEK_EDYNAMO

     Amount $24.78

     + Tip: _____

     = Total: _____

X_____

     HARLOW MORGAN

     Customer Copy

     Greenlake Grill
7200 East Green Lake Dr N
   Seattle, Wa 98115
    206-729-6179

and prefacing the meanness by disclaiming it was ridiculous. But I hear it all the time, "I'm not saying this to be a jerk, but ..." or "I don't want to hurt your feelings, but ..." and all of the good intentions to *not* be hurtful are negated by the criticism that follows. Feedback given with love and without criticism, offered only if asked, is necessary in a relationship. Criticism will destroy it. Be clear on this: *there is no such thing as constructive criticism.*

Codependents are plagued with fear. We believe that, as I did for many years, if we do everything right and make sure that everyone else does everything right (meaning the way we want them to), we will avoid the pain of loss. We enter into relationships with damaged or emotionally unavailable partners, thinking we can fill the hole that the scars of their childhood left. We believe that we need this person to love us. We need him or her because somewhere in there we believe that being loved by this person will validate us and clear up all of those unpleasant insecurities we developed early in life. We believe that if we are pretty enough, smart enough, funny enough, sexy enough, successful enough, etc., the other person will see our value and will love us the way that we want to be loved, and we will feel complete. This is simply wrong thinking.

The way your partner treats you is the way he or she treats others in a relationship. It is not personal. It has very little to do with you. If you tolerate being mistreated, and you have chosen to stay in a relationship in which you are mistreated, there is nothing to be gained by blaming your partner except possible sympathy from others. If you stand up for yourself and state that you are not willing to stay in a relationship in which you are mistreated, the other person has a choice. You cannot change that person. If that person agrees that he or she needs to change, then perhaps it will happen. If it doesn't and you stay, you have chosen to be mistreated. I do not intend to blame the victims of physically abusive relationships. There is real danger to an abused partner who threatens to leave. There is no easy choice in that situation, and it is important to seek professional help.

Here is how fear worked in my life.

I was all about control. I wanted the towels folded in thirds, the dishwasher loaded efficiently, the weeds pulled from the lawn, the toilet paper hanging down the front of the roll. Anyone who tried to help me would get subtly insulted because I had to go quietly behind them and do it my way. I was the expert at my home and my children's lives. I thought I was an expert at my life, but as you will see, I had no clue. I thought I knew how to ensure my children's success and happiness. I thought that I could protect them from pain. I thought I knew their needs.

Molly, the youngest of three, was the easy one. As an infant she loved her crib and settled in for naps with a comfortable sigh, whereas my two older children were coaxed to sleep with rocking and songs, stories and backrubs. Looking back I wonder if I wasn't just bothering them so much that they couldn't have fallen asleep!

Molly was a happy little girl. She was the people-pleaser in the family. She made friends with anyone in proximity. She loved to sing, dance, and play act fantasy scenarios. One evening in the backyard when she was four years old, Molly leaned back in her swing and started singing softly as she gazed into the heavens:

"Pretty, pretty night.

I wonder what it is.

Stars up in the sky

I wonder what it is."

Her father and I stood bewitched in silence. It was a magical moment. One of so many.

Turning the car radio to full-blast, she would sing along and invite everyone to sing with her. I loved it and sang loud, with her. Even when she discovered that it was embarrassing to be driven around by a mother, she loved singing together in the car.

Her dad and I divorced … an amicable agreement, if there is such a thing when you sever what had seemed like one life into two. Our children suffered nevertheless, each spiraling into their own silent misery.

I watched Molly as she transformed from a pretty girl into a stunning young woman before our eyes. She learned about haircuts and facial hair removal and clothes that fit perfectly. She learned how to walk and how to flirt. What had been innocent fantasy-play in her childhood morphed into romantic drama. It was scary. She needed something that I could not give her.

My fear was out of control. She was fifteen and in high school when the older boys started coming around. I wanted to build a moat around my home. Around my daughter. I wanted to lock her in a tower until the tom-cats quit howling. I tried hard to control the situation. We made rules. The harder we tried to control her world, the more she hid from us. Her music became dark and demeaning.

I received the phone call as I was leaving my office to teach an early morning class at a small local university. She had shot herself.

I raced to the emergency room. She was only fifteen. It seemed like forever before the receptionist finally took me back to the ER. Molly's father was talking to a physician. The looks on their faces said it all.

The events of the previous evening had been humiliating to her. She had been caught in a lie about an older boy who had shown up at her father's house late one night. The scene had been ugly. Her father never knew how his gun ended up in her hand.

Molly was gone. I loved her with all of my heart and still do. She had felt complete hopelessness and like any fifteen-year-old could not conceive that the misery was only temporary.

I remember very little of the next four years, except sitting on the couch in my den with my devastated two children, day after day, week after week, going through the motions. We got a kitten that was able to help us smile. We sat and watched her shred the curtains from top to bottom, without the energy or care to stop her.

My fear had been about drugs or sex or Molly not realizing what a precious, amazing woman she was. My fear had been about some older boy taking this precious woman away and hurting her. My fear had been about predators and crazy adolescent thinking.

In my fear I had so expertly tried to control her life and rescue her from pain that I had not given her the tools to survive adolescence. One day she was showing me pictures of the car of her dreams, hoping that someday she would have that car. The next day she was dead.

My fear had done nothing for me or for her. It stunted my family. My fear was about trying to avoid fear. Fear is only powerful if it is denied or avoided, in which case it will be acted out negatively. A life lived trying to avoid fear is completely futile.

Fear keeps us focused on ourselves instead of attending to others.

Growth comes from walking through fear.

I now had to walk through my fear of living with my daughter's suicide. Forever. No way out. I had to walk through it or perish, quite literally. I had to learn how to parent my near-adult, deeply wounded surviving children (ages seventeen and eighteen when their sister died). I let go of control. I let go of fear. I had experienced the worst possible pain, and no problem, however big could create pain that would compare to facing a life with only the memory of a dear, sweet child who chose to end her life.

Love

> Your task is not to seek for love, but merely to seek and find all
> the barriers within yourself that you have built against it.
> —Rumi

All positive emotions are love-based. This is easier to grasp. What is difficult is figuring out what love really means.

Love is complete acceptance of self and others, with the courage to hold your loved ones to behavior that dignifies their person. It means allowing them the opportunity to experience the natural consequences of their actions and loving them through the learning process, even when the natural consequence requires that you love them from a distance.

I like the word *cherish*. Criticism is not an act of love. We can only truly love another person if we embrace the totality of him or her. We love our addicted children when we accept that they are who they are, and that we cannot carve out the addict and only love the healthy, easy child. We create the structure and consequences for them to find their way to health, but the journey is theirs.

Although it sounds cliché, it is true that you must love yourself before you have love to give. How can you offer a commodity of which you have none? Without self-acceptance, we tend to focus within and attend to how others see us. When that is no longer an issue, we can just love others without judging them and can choose the closeness of the relationship or the distance.

It is an act of love to light up the room with your smile when you see your child. It is also an act of love to allow her to fail and feel the growth and confidence that comes from realizing the extent to which she controls her own destiny. Some parents panic and cannot trust their child to negotiate the pain of failure, which sends a clear message that you believe the child is incompetent.

Most families who are new to recovery begin their journey in fear and anger. If they do this work, they find that they are soon filled with love. They are able to talk to each other with honesty and directness and are in awe of each other's uniqueness. They learn that parenting from fear leaves them angry, resentful, and terrified. Their anger with each other and anger with their child comes from their fear that their child will not survive. When they learn how to love, and to love each other, they are able to reunite as a family and to keep healthy boundaries in place.

If you approach life with love, you are able to respond rather than react to the things going on around you. Susan called me, panicked because her sixteen-year-old daughter had relapsed and had not come home for two nights. In the absence of real information, she had been carried by her fear directly to the ultimate parent-nightmare—dead in a ditch. If she reacted out of fear, she would probably have gotten in her car and driven all over town, banging on doors and calling hospitals. This was a wonderful opportunity for both Susan and her daughter to turn things around. Reacting out of fear would rob them both of this opportunity.

Instead, she made a loving plan that respected her daughter's need to learn from her relapse and her need to take care of herself. She called the police to report the child as a runaway. She called her sponsor and went to a meeting. She checked out a residential treatment center for the availability of a bed, insurance coverage, etc., packed a small bag for her daughter, and acknowledged her powerlessness over her daughter's behavior. She waited.

Her daughter returned after four days, as if nothing had happened. Her mom cried and hugged her, grateful to see that she was alive. Her daughter thought Susan was being overly dramatic and tried to push past her to go to her room. Susan stated two options: go to residential treatment or move out of her home (see Rules and Consequences). The daughter exploded. How dare her mother try to control her like that? Susan knew that she couldn't control her if she tried. Susan could provide a safe environment for her daughter to begin getting help for her problems. Susan could participate in a program for parents. If her daughter needed to go on living like she had been, it would break Susan's heart, but she had no control over her.

What Susan could control was how she was willing to live in her own home. She could refuse to watch her child self-destruct, which is very different from trying to stop the behavior. She could refuse to provide her daughter a comfortable place to destroy her life, which is very different from trying to control her daughter's behavior by allowing her the comfort of home. Her daughter was given the choice: she could get in the car or run off without any personal belongings. Her daughter rolled her eyes, started walking to her room, and said she would think about it but that she was tired and needed to sleep. Susan lovingly said that she could sleep in the car but that her daughter's options that involved Susan's home were not open for further discussion. Her daughter stormed out of the house, slammed the door, and was gone. In several hours, the girl returned home and to Susan's complete shock, got in the car.

This was the natural consequence of her daughter's drug use. The only long-term options for the addict are death, incarceration, insanity (usually homelessness), or to make the choice and do the work to recover. The addict cannot keep using without an enabler to keep them somewhat comfortable. Susan was not willing to be the enabler.

If she had been operating out of fear, Susan would have let her daughter go to her room to sleep when she returned after being missing. She would have taken her a mug of warm soup, had a nice chat, asked the girl to go to treatment, and lived in worry and fear. The girl wouldn't have appreciated her mother's kindness or her pain. She would leave again on a whim. Susan's fear could have endangered her daughter, but instead she felt it and walked through it. Enabling is self-serving, the most unloving position one can take, and yet it feels like love.

Love, Fear, and Ego

> If you want to awaken all of humanity, then awaken all of
> yourself, if you want to eliminate the suffering in the world,
> then eliminate all that is negative in yourself. Truly, the greatest
> gift you have to give is that of your own self-transformation.
> —Lao Tzu

We cannot move toward a solution if the problem is masked by self-protective egos. Fear is ego-protective. Our fear points us toward opportunities to grow. The way to conquer fear is to dissolve its illusion of realness. We call this walking through fear. Fear is in our heads. When in the face of fear, we take a deep breath and continue on, and we grow. Courage isn't the fearlessness of superheroes; it is the willingness to say the hard things, do the right things, and take the necessary risks in spite of our fear.

Michael Mendizza (2004) describes the disruption of relationship that occurs when parents allow their fears and insecurities to override the bond between them and their child:

> We can't really see and respond to others as they are while looking out for our agenda, our self-interests. (p. 6)

We let our egos get woven into our parenting. We let our child's success become our own. We are proud. Then of course their problems become our own. We are ashamed. Our shame becomes their shame.

This is self-centered thinking, and must be set aside in order to become effective. At this point, you are where you are. It does not matter who did what to get you here. What matters is where you go from here. You have choices. Your life is now, in this one moment, the culmination of every decision you have made. Look with gut-wrenching honesty at your behavior. If you have made your life someone else's responsibility, you cannot get your power back unless you realize that you gave it away. If you cannot look with kind and gentle clarity into your actions, you cannot know yourself. You cannot love that which you do not know. If you have been putting up a front, hiding your true self, making impressions, and hoping to be seen as perfect, no one can love you because they do not know who you are. They can love the illusion. They can only love you if you expose your magnificent imperfection.

If a person is mean or judgmental, it is because he or she is mean and judgmental. This person has been damaged and has work to do in order to become whole and loving. It has nothing to do with you. Do not waste time trying to please a person who is mean and judgmental. Every ounce of emotional effort spent trying to get someone to love you the way you want them to love you in spite of their consistent behavior to the contrary is useless. You can love them at arm's length, but you cannot please them and they cannot love you because they can only be who they are, and they will either be open to a loving relationship or not.

> The beginning of love is to let those we love be perfectly themselves, and not to twist them to fit our own image. Otherwise we love only the reflection of ourselves we find in them.
> —Thomas Merton

Chapter 12

SPIRITUALITY AND FORGIVENESS

The spiritual journey is individual, highly personal. It can't be organized or regulated. It isn't true that everyone should follow one path. Listen to your own truth.
—Ram Dass

Many of the teens I have known completely rejected the idea of a higher power at some point along the way. How could such a being allow their lives to become such a disaster filled with such pain? If they ever did believe in God, they now mistrust him or deny him. Their parents also may feel that God has abandoned them. What kind of God, after all of my loyalty and service, would allow this to happen to my child? What kind of God would allow this incredibly sick and dangerous culture that destroys children to exist among his own creations? Why does he not just save our child?

It is easy to feel rejected and abandoned by God. How can you now believe in, trust, and invest in a relationship with this God? These are real and valid feelings.

What I have come to believe is that none of us is alone. We are a community of souls in a life that we cannot negotiate without each other. The fellowship of man is powerful. If there is no God, then each of us is aimlessly spinning our wheels in a meaningless existence only to perish into dust. We get to choose.

If there is no power outside of ourselves, how can we feel such deep love for our children? For each other? If there is not some force that is greater than myself, why do I feel joy at a sunset, love for the elderly stranger selecting an apple from a bin? How can we feel such despair when torn from those we love if there isn't something more powerful than ourselves? Are love and joy no more than biological artifacts of patterns of neurons firing? If so, why is there something palpable going on in a room full of people with common interests? If so, why do we care what others think or feel, what they are doing or not doing? We are connected by something.

I once heard a seventeen-year-old boy, recovering from addiction to heroin, say that he had once believed that no one could love him and that he was alone. He felt that not only was he unlovable by others, but there was no way that he could tolerate himself without numbing his feelings. He came into the fellowship of a twelve-step program and was loved unconditionally. Nobody believed his lies, and nobody was willing to be manipulated by him, and still everyone in his community loved him patiently until he slowly began to trust the love. He eventually was able to love himself. Then the miracle happened. He felt something new. He could love others. The thing that had been missing all along, he said, was his ability to give love, not that no one loved him. The good feelings are in the giving of love.

There is love and there is fear. All things good come from love. All misery comes from fear. We are constantly turning either toward the light or away from it. When we turn away from it, we begin to fear, we get jealous, and we experience bitterness and resentment. We get judgmental. Love is a shared experience. Love is about being connected, and in that connectedness spirituality thrives. Some call it God, some call it a higher power. It doesn't matter what you call it. It brings peace.

Fear is a solitary experience. Anger, jealousy, and criticism are all lonely experiences that kill any hope of connectedness or spiritual existence.

Resentment

Most of us have a person or persons in our past who have hurt us. We were mistreated, abused, abandoned, judged, shamed, and scarred by our experiences with this person or persons. We blame them. We detest them. We hold on to this negativity, and it holds permanent residence in our emotions. Nelson Mandela said this of resentment: "Resentment is like drinking poison and hoping that your enemy will die."

Most resentment stems from one of two issues: unrealistic expectations and failure to set boundaries.

Unrealistic Expectations

When asked, most of us do not even want to forgive the offender because he or she doesn't deserve it. We still feel that we need something from them—atonement or humility or the experience of angst over the pain they have caused. This is not likely to happen. We had an expectation that we thought was reasonable. We discovered that this other person didn't see things the way that we see them and did not fulfill our expectation.

We expect our fathers to be the attentive and loving father for whom we long. We expect our mothers to be as we fantasize the perfect mother. We expect our children to respect and love us. We expect our teachers to be infallible.

Fathers, mothers, children, and all people in the important roles in our lives are imperfect. They do as they have learned to do. Fathers who work compulsively discount the value of their marriage and neglect the children, believing they are doing what they are supposed to do. Mothers who attempt to balance careers and home life try to be all things to all people and neglect their own needs. Children trying to negotiate a culture that is foreign to their parents get lost in the social maelstrom and lose faith in their parents' ability to help them. No one means harm. Everyone falls short of others' expectations. The boundaries get blurry. Mistakes are made. There is pain. Do we carry the resentments of our disappointment forever? At what point do we set aside our expectations that this person who has never treated us as we hoped they would will somehow miraculously "get it" and be who we want them to be?

As adults, hopefully we have developed empathy. We can actually, if we are willing, imagine the relationship from the other person's perspective, through the lens of his or her experiences and opinions. If today someone doesn't treat you as you wish, then he or she probably won't treat you differently tomorrow. Don't set yourself up to be hurt. Don't set the other person up to fail. Give up the expectation. You are an adult, and now you have the chance to free yourself from the misery of resentment. If that other person cannot treat you as you wish, he or she cannot. You can't make him or her fulfill your expectations.

Somehow we tend to want them to see what they have done that hurt us. We want them to suffer as we have suffered and to acknowledge that they were wrong.

Who is losing sleep over this? Who is feeling that resentment well up inside, doing damage to internal organs and systems? Who is angry and disappointed long after the damage is done? Whose relationships are tarnished by the negativity we carry? It isn't the perpetrator. It is you and me.

When our resentment is damaging to our bodies and spirits, when we identify as victims and cannot free ourselves from this mentality, when we honor our perpetrator with countless hours of ruminating and describing to others how we have been mistreated, building a case for our victim-hood, this is when we may realize the need to unburden ourselves.

The deeds of the past cannot be changed. Every positive day in our lives becomes one more piece of a better past with tomorrow's sunrise. We change our perception of the past when we take ownership of the misery and stop letting it ruin our present lives.

For many of us, these feelings are about our abusive parents, our selfish or cruel ex-spouses, our unreasonable employers, or persons in whom we placed trust but who did not fulfill our expectations. Every person has a history that has influenced his or her acts. Every person has a story.

Unset Boundaries

We get hurt when people mistreat us. Sometimes we are caught off guard. Sometimes we see it coming but can't seem to stop it. Sometimes it seems so obvious that we fail to actually articulate our discomfort. I see this in adolescents all of the time. Someone they trust or admire teases them, playfully, sometimes strategically. They laugh and go along with it. They know that if they fight it the teasing will be worse. Girls are notorious for allowing boys to tickle and grope them while giggling and saying, "Stop it!" in a voice that seems to be enjoying the fun. They aren't taken seriously, and later they are resentful. This is a great opportunity for them to learn to stand up for themselves like an adult and say with seriousness and clarity that they will not tolerate uninvited touching and will without hesitation end a relationship with any person who disrespects this boundary.

Cassandra's father wants more of her time, but she is sixteen years old, and although she loves him, she just isn't interested in the things that he likes to do and is always on her phone. He expects her to be ready to talk to him, which she experiences as listening to him, every day when he comes home from work. She doesn't want to hurt his feelings, so she goes along with his wishes but then uses her phone to make it more tolerable. He is always offended. She has become resentful of these "talks" and tries to find ways to avoid them. She doesn't want him to be hurt, so she tries to justify her actions. One of these days she will outright tell him that she would love to spend time with him but that his expectations are unreasonable. Perhaps they could do something that she wants to do once a month, or maybe he could show an interest in the things that she is involved in without expressing his opinions and criticism. She may someday tell him that she wants a relationship but that it feels to her like he only wants an audience. This simple boundary, although it will take courage to set, will prevent an explosion of resentment down the road when as an adult she lives with her disappointment that he was never really interested in her and never accepted who she is as a person.

There are countless mothers out there, and as many fathers, who have done everything they possibly could for their child and absolutely cannot seem to get the kid to do a simple chore for them. The parents' failure to set firm boundaries around acceptable behavior, participation in the family, and respect for their family members have set them up to resent their child.

Of course the boundaries that need to be set in an abusive relationship are crucial for emotional if not physical survival. Emotional abuse has to be stopped the very first time it occurs with the expression of a firm statement backed up with willingness to follow through with action. A person who is abusive will not stop if you express your misery but do not leave. If you express yourself and then leave when the abuse recurs, you never have to be abused again. You cannot change that person. If you are being physically abused and fear that you will be in danger if you leave, you will need to get professional help and a support group. You are absolutely correct in your assessment of the danger you are in.

So often, we find ourselves in relationships in which we feel that we are being used or taken for granted. To set a boundary, we voice our concern, stating the limits beyond which we cannot tolerate the other person's behavior. In most cases, the other adult will respond with genuine effort to understand and adjust his or her behavior, not wanting to hurt us. If we hope that the statement of our boundary will in itself change the other person's treatment of us, we may be setting ourselves up for resentment. We have to recognize that the other person may not change and that we then have the choice to stay or go. If we stay, we have made the choice to develop resentment, and it will hurt us, not the other person.

Forgiveness

> When you judge another, you do not define them,
> you define yourself.
> —Wayne Dyer

The person who hurt you will lose his or her grip on your life when you simply forgive the misdeed. Forgiveness means that you no longer blame. You are no longer a victim. You are the owner of your soul and your life. You have choices. You never have to be hurt by that person again. By holding the resentment, you allow that wound to perpetuate and fester. You give the perpetrator the power over your happiness and emotional stability.

Forgiveness is not about letting the other person off the hook. You do not have to like or further tolerate what they have done that caused pain to forgive them. You do not have to maintain a relationship with that person.

Visualize that person as a child. The child is hurt. The child learns lessons just as you have, about how to act in the world, what to believe, who to trust, and what to expect from others. They learn what they learn. They are who they are. Usually they feel that they are justified in their actions.

The only way to maintain a relationship with a person who has hurt you is to change your expectations of his or her behavior or set some clear boundaries. We can maintain a relationship with family members who have been mean or cruel by giving up the need for them to love us the way we want. If they are mean or cruel, it is because they are mean or cruel for whatever reasons, not because there is something wrong with you. This is critical to understand if that person is your child. Your child did not do this *to you*. Your child's addiction drives bad behavior.

They are who they are, and they pay the price.

You cannot trust them, confide in them, take their advice, or turn to them when you need help. You must protect yourself. You can perhaps eventually have dinner with them and laugh at their jokes and recognize the boundaries and expectations that the relationship requires.

Forgiving that person means that you understand his or her limits. You do not have to like them, and you do not have to tolerate them, but you are no longer going to go through life being their victim. When you forgive, you make the choice to protect yourself from any further mistreatment and give up the idea of trying to change the offender.

You do not have to articulate your forgiveness to this person. You do not need to reunite with this person. You do not need to open yourself to further hurt. Now you are in charge of your life, and now you can anticipate and protect yourself before the abuse happens.

An adult who has hurt you has grown up into an imperfect adult, like you and me. He or she makes mistakes and is immature or selfish at times. He or she might repeat those mistakes and continue to hurt others. This is a sad reality, but it does not need to take up space in my life or yours. That person may not deserve your forgiveness, but you deserve the comfort that lies in letting go by forgiving.

Forgiveness is easy if the person who hurt you comes to you and acknowledges their mistreatment of you. This is rare. I don't recommend that you wait for this to happen. If you feel that you need that person to understand and acknowledge your pain, you must release that need in order to forgive. By clinging to this irrational need you only prolong your misery.

Sitting quietly, it is possible to choose to allow the lightness of love to flow through your body. As if the air that we breathe is pure and unconditionally accepting love, breathe it in and feel the peace that is available when we turn from the misery. Imagine the love flowing from you to others and then beyond. Breathe out the impure air, as if releasing all of the need you have been carrying—the need for that person to be as you had wanted. Release your need and you can forgive and let go of the expectations, and you will no longer be hurt. From this position, I can wish the best for them, sometimes from a distance. It may not be immediate, because you have to train your brain to let it go, but you will get there if you practice.

Forgive your children and your parents. Forgive those whose actions are continuing to run your emotions and prevent your contentment. Feel the love. Above all, love and forgive yourself.

Family Recovery Stories

The following are stories that have been sent to me by parents and teens who have completed the Cornerstone program in Houston, where I worked as I wrote this book.

You hear everywhere that addiction is an equal-opportunity disease. The parents in this program are of many faiths, many fields of work, a wide range of socioeconomic circumstances, many ages, some divorced but most married, some gay or lesbian, a widely varied cultural heritage and race, and some of the most loving and dedicated parents you would ever hope to know.

I am grateful that they are willing to allow me to publish their stories, which have all been slightly adjusted to protect their identities.

We Thought We Were in Control

Our family story began when our son was just about sixteen, nine years ago. He was the kid you would want your kid to have as a friend. A strong Christian, close to our family, kindhearted, selfless, in the gifted program at school, creative and musically talented, on the select sports teams, and had a great group of friends. Sounds almost perfect, right? Obviously, it wasn't inside his heart. He was a quiet, very sensitive person who was hurt easily. Even with all the accomplishments, his belief in himself was low. We would encourage and try to build him up with the truth, but he didn't believe our words. We would hear from the teachers, "I wish I had a whole classroom of him!" That sounded terrific, but the root of that was he craved approval, self-esteem, and perfection.

At the end of middle school, his very best friend moved away. Eventually he found a new group of friends, some of which we were not pleased about. The changes in him began. His grades were still good and he even had a job, but we started to see erratic behavior. We thought he had anxiety, so he began medication. He was still not happy, he was gone more, and when at home, he was in his room. We knew something was wrong. He and his new group were caught doing things that were totally *not* our son. Let me say we now know it was not the new friends' fault. Our son did these things by choice, but later in the program we saw how essential healthy peers are to recovery.

Not too long after that, our son came to me deeply upset and crying. I tried desperately to remain calm and prayed "Help" to God. Through his tears, he told me that for almost a year he had been smoking marijuana. He tried many times to quit but couldn't. It was ruining his life, and he begged for help to stop. I was in complete shock. Never, ever would I have expected that from him. I turned on my "codependency fix-it mode" and told him we would stop this and fix it. I promised! The next day I was on the phone with a private counselor getting him an appointment and "fixing" everything. We went into over-control, actually thinking we could keep him safe. We put him on lockdown. He could only go to school and his job—the safe places (right)—and no more of those "friends." A little time passed, but he seemed more depressed and erratic. He finally came to us and said he was still smoking at school and with his coworkers—the very places we considered safe! Oh, how naïve my husband and I had been! We had no idea what to do.

Completely out of the blue, we met a man who was participating with his daughter in an alternative peer group. We had no idea what that was, but he was very sincere about how much better things had gotten in this program. We decided to go.

We walked in scared, in deep pain, and feeling like horrible parents. We had our "newcomers meeting" with the most wonderful, beautiful woman who was another parent in the program. She shared many of our values and fears. We could feel the kindness and concern from her. She was a huge part of why we stayed.

The kids in the group looked like the kids we had always tried to avoid. We were skeptical. But the other parents reassured us, and after actually talking to the kids we felt okay about his new friends.

The staff member we talked to was so blunt—I hated it. He said we had to let go and let him own his recovery and do it himself. Oh, how I fought it. I wanted to make sure he was doing it and that this problem would be solved. I didn't trust that he could or would do it without me. It was my fear that kept our family from progressing for the first few months. Then this same staff member had the audacity to tell us we had to work on ourselves too. What? My husband and I weren't addicts. We didn't need recovery. Work a program? We would go to meetings, learn about this problem and support our son, but we didn't need a program! What was this pushy, video game–playing guy talking about??

My husband, son, and I immersed ourselves into the program. Our son went through an intensive outpatient program and incessantly hung out with the other kids in the group. It seemed like we never saw him, but when we did, he looked happier. My husband and I lived in the car driving to the meetings in Houston and our small Kingwood meeting. We went to functions, coffees, and step-studies, became part of leadership, became sponsors—we did it all! We laughed, cried, hugged, and said "luv ya" a lot! We were so hungry for the unconditional love, fellowship, and education. We made lifetime friends. We would do anything to help our son heal, but it fed us as well. Our lives were all about Cornerstone because that is where we needed to be!

Our son became a leader in the program, but his recovery wasn't perfect. He had some tough times, but we knew what to do.

He went on to community college and earned scholarships to different schools. He chose the University of Houston and remained close to the supportive group of friends in his recovery circle. He graduated summa cum laude with an accounting degree and started working for an accounting firm two days after graduation. He has been truly successful in life. He, of course, has a job, but he is happy, has self-esteem, has integrity, and is incredibly loving and humble. His best friends are still those peers from his recovery program. He has been clean and sober for many years, and *he* owns it, not us!

My husband and I continue to live the principles of recovery to guide us personally, along with our deep faith in God as well.

I Was Sure I Knew Best

I heard recently that there are eighty-six thousand seconds in a day—that makes a day seem a lot longer than twenty-four hours. I can't even begin to imagine how many seconds that means I've lived—but there's a lot of zeros behind that number of seconds, and some of those seconds were long, hard seconds in the midst of the destruction and dysfunction in our family over our daughter's addiction.

If someone had told me all that would happen in the past five years I would definitely *not* have thought it good that my daughter would be an alcoholic and her disease would bring us to the door steps of a place called Cornerstone. Today I can honestly say it has been a good thing, a blessing to have a child who would push us into a program that has provided more than we could have ever dreamed.

I'm the oldest of three girls, and both my parents are alcoholics. Their disease was hidden within our dysfunctional family for a long time, and it adversely affected my sisters and me, as it does all children of alcoholics. Unfortunately I had no interest in getting involved in any type of recovery like Al-Anon in my early adulthood. I felt then that the more distance I could put between my parents' alcoholism and my life as an adult, the better things would be. Of course I now know you can't run away from the dysfunctions or the defects in yourself; you merely carry them with you into all your relationships. I brought my own dysfunctions and defects full blown into my marriage, and it also colored my parenting skills.

I was a controlling parent, a real helicopter parent actually. Our daughter was headstrong and stubborn, but I knew that if I was a good enough parent and involved enough in her life, I could keep her from falling into the wrong crowd and making big mistakes. This was wrong, of course.

When things got bad enough, we sent her to residential treatment and felt sure when she returned after eight and a half months in Utah, she would be fixed. We came to Cornerstone for aftercare, but we really weren't convinced it was totally necessary. We thought she would be able to keep all her friends from the past and still stay in recovery.

We were so mistaken. After only a few weeks home, she relapsed, and we realized then how necessary aftercare might be. It made no sense to me that Cornerstone would be able to help our child after eight and a half months in residential treatment had failed. I was so wrong. I certainly had no reason to believe that I needed help, although I strongly suspected my husband did.

I was skeptical and upset at first to have to attend parent meetings twice a week and parenting group every Monday night. However, I felt like a complete failure as a parent and was willing to give it a try so I came with my notebook and pen in hand ready to figure out how to fix my child.

What I learned very quickly was that I needed to fix myself and quit trying to control my daughter! This was a novel ideal for sure, one I had never thought of and really didn't trust at first. For sure I didn't like hearing that I was expected to do the twelve steps, get a sponsor, and participate in a step study. What I really wanted to do was beat up on the counselors to fix my daughter (which I often did) and then get on with our lives and leave Cornerstone behind! So my own recovery didn't really start until we came to Cornerstone, which was specifically to get our daughter "fixed."

Finally after a few months, I gave in. I started writing in my notebook how to work on myself, and that's when my recovery began. I slowly started to identify with this weird collection of codependent, enabling parents. I didn't always understand what was said, but I could see they had been through similar pain and now had joy, and I wanted it. I did the work.

I now possess that joy, peace, and serenity, and no matter what choices my daughter makes in the future, I know how to get it. It's not that I didn't know the source of my strength before, but I didn't trust fully when it came to my daughter. I was certainly a "Mother knows best" codependent.

I still feel like I often know what's best for my daughter, yet I've learned to stop trying to control her or the outcomes and allow her to deal with her choices and the consequences that may come from those choices. This has made our relationship so much healthier and so much better than ever before.

I've learned some tools in this program that are invaluable like:

- "Detaching with love" does not mean disengaging from the relationship.
- "Letting go and letting God" means that I can't control anyone but me, so I have to quit worrying about everything and everyone else.
- "Practice makes progress" means that no skill is developed overnight, and we only need to keep growing, not to become perfect.
- "Codependency kills" means exactly that—taking away another person's ability to grow is damaging.
- "Live in the moment" means that yesterday got me here and today is taking me somewhere. If I don't pay attention to today, I may end up somewhere I don't want to be.
- We were always powerless, but our codependency gave us the illusion of control.

I've found friends for life and have an even stronger marriage and relationship with my husband. That daughter I wanted to get "fixed"— well, I now have a daughter who is working an incredible program of recovery. She is brave, smart, self-confident, a good mentor and sponsor, and an inspiration to others. She is honest, trustworthy, spiritually grounded, and beautiful inside and out, and she has a very promising future.

Our Kids Would Never Drink

My grandfather on my mother's side died on the street in his hometown. Alcoholism was passed down through many generations on both sides of the family. Both of my parents were alcoholics.

There was violence in our house: physical, spiritual, emotional, and sexual. Mom was humiliated by Dad's involvement with other women. My dad used my mom's drinking as an excuse. His raging created a war zone, and each of us reacted with fear, anger, rage, terror, and resentment.

I stayed home from school a lot to take care of my mom. I was supposed to keep her from drinking. Our home and my life were full of secrets that we could not tell anyone. I did not know what the truth was. I thought it was my job to make everybody okay. I was terrified of my dad and tried to keep out of his way and was constantly worried that my mom was going to die or my dad would kill her.

I started drinking when I was sixteen, and for the first time I felt comfortable in my own skin. I could laugh, talk to people, and get attention that I desperately wanted. All I wanted was to numb the pain and find someone to love me. I hung out in unhealthy places with unhealthy people like myself and was always in trouble.

My mother's frequent overdoses, hospitalizations, and treatment admissions distracted everyone in the family. They never noticed my drinking, just my behavior. I never put it together that my behavior and my drinking went hand in hand. I would lie to my parents about who I was with and where I was going. Eventually drinking did not work so well. I began to feel ashamed.

My dad went to jail at one point for choking my mom. I continued to drink all the way into my first marriage. My husband and I began fighting over other women. We fought. We drank. The patterns were repeating.

My dad got cancer that spread to his brain. My mom stole and used my dad's morphine. My marriage was out of control. I could not handle my husband's drinking and my parents' dysfunction. I realized that I could not hang on to the belief that I could fix it any more. I was at my bottom. With some help from my sister, I got into Al-Anon and began to learn about the disease and my codependency. A few years later I got sober. I stayed married for five more years before I finally was sick and tired of being sick and tired. I ask my husband to leave.

My dad passed away, and I continued to go to meetings and work the program. I began to build my self-esteem and friendships in the program. God was doing for me what I could not do for myself. My mother got sober, and I was elated. I was so desperate for my mother. We went to all kinds of meetings and conventions together, had slumber parties, and shared our recovery friends. Mom lived the last ten years of her life sober, as my confidante and friend. We prayed together, and we healed together. I thank God for my mother and the sober motherly moments she gave to me.

I met my second husband, in AA. This was the beginning of a new life. We would be really involved in our twelve-step programs, live a life of recovery, and be examples for our kids. We had a daughter. I never wanted her to live with active addiction or feel the way I felt growing up. I wanted to protect her from hurting or being hurt. I always put her needs first. I felt like being a parent was something I always wanted to do and was good at.

I really did not understand how to parent or to be consistent. I did not really understand the importance of accountability or letting her fail. I think I hated my own imperfection and wanted my daughter to be perfect. I also wanted to be her friend like my mom was for me in those last years. She started getting in trouble in high school; Saturday detentions, stealing, lying to us, and hanging out with kids we didn't approve of. She locked herself in her room when she was home and was always angry. I was afraid of her.

My husband and I didn't agree on how to parent. He thought I was too hard on her, and I thought he was such a pushover that he was the problem. We were fighting all the time. He and I were never on the same page about most things, and we continued to fight. I thought she was just rebellious, and I grounded her for long periods at a time. I did not know how to help her. I would lay awake at night and worry about her. I began checking her phone and calling her friends' parents. I'd search her room, looking for clues to what was going on. I was not able to get her to do the most basic things, like get to school on time. I resented her for not appreciating me. I was powerless and terrified.

In March of 2010, one of her friend's parents called to let us know that they had found their daughter blacked out in a field the night before. I realized that my daughter was probably drinking as well. I had lived in this fantasy that my child would never have to drink, and I never put it together that she had been drinking, much less using drugs as well. I confronted her and told her she was going to an AA meeting with me. She went, and at that meeting, three girls from Cornerstone came up after the meeting and introduced themselves to us and asked my daughter if she had a problem. She didn't say anything, so I told them that something was clearly wrong. They invited her to Cornerstone the next night. Her father took her to her first meeting, and I went along the following week.

We all became very involved in the program. I thought I was already working a twelve-step program and didn't need to "work the program," but I soon learned that I had never worked the serious kind of program that this group encouraged. I got a sponsor, attended the functions, hosted kids, worked the steps, and went to the meetings. My husband and I worked hard to create a unified front, and I quit blaming him. We quit fighting and focused on our own health and boundaries instead of arguing over our daughter's. I began to feel hope. I no longer felt alone. I saw how other parents felt the way I felt and did what I did. I learned how to love and respect myself and take my power back. I learned how to parent effectively. I learned that love meant not accepting wrong behavior. I learned to forgive myself and my daughter. I learned to laugh with her, cry with her, and have fun with her. I learned how important it was for her to make mistakes and find her own way. I learned to trust her again, and more important I learned to trust me.

Today I have taken my life back and enjoy the talents and gifts God has given me. The promises have all come true on so many levels. God is doing for me what I cannot do for myself. I am so grateful to God and this program for the beginning of a whole new way of life and the tools that are necessary for my growth and the growth of my family.

Of Course, I Wasn't Codependent

I came into the program in May 2009, just before the summer wilderness trip. My first meeting was a parent/kid meeting, and I was nervous and excited about being there. I wanted something to hope for and was really grateful for the warm reception both me and my daughter received when we walked in—especially my daughter.

She was sixteen and had just completed an outpatient program in Clear Lake after several trips to a psychiatric hospital the prior year. At fifteen she was cutting, disrespectful, dramatic, depressed, acting out, making poor grades, and getting in trouble at school functions.

Typical of me, I was going to find the reason behind her issues and find the solution. We spent a year and a half going from therapist to psychiatrist to hospitals and treatment facilities. I found out during intake at a psychiatric hospital that she had been heavily involved in drugs. I thought she was exaggerating the extent of her drug use like everything else! But even if she only used half as much as she admitted, we had a huge problem. I felt mentally and physically exhausted.

We started attending the Cornerstone program, totally dependent on help from the families who greeted and reached out to us. Sending her off with a car full of sober girls to girls' night was a welcome relief. I felt like she had found a welcoming group unlike any other group she had been part of. I hung around in the pink cloud for a while, thinking she was healing, and of course I didn't have a problem! We were fixed.

After four months, she and her boyfriend broke up. She took a handful of Trazadone, and I drove her to the emergency room. The attempt was a shock to both of us. She spent a month at a psychiatric facility in San Antonio. This was the wake-up call that we both really needed to do some work.

While she was gone, I got an amazing sponsor and dove into the parent program. I read many of the recommended books for new parents. It felt different going through this with other people who understood, cared, and gave me constructive ideas, not just to deal with the situation at hand but to see it with new eyes—a new perspective. This time, the whole world wasn't on my shoulders, and I finally started to get it.

I recall being in meetings and seeing flyers. I picked up the one on codependence. Of course, I wasn't co-dependent ... that was a role my mother played with my brothers, not me. I was blown away that everything I read was totally describing me. It was like a jolt seeing myself described so accurately with the title "codependent" attached to it!

My daughter came back and slowly committed to the Cornerstone program. We met with a staff member who discussed all of the available activities, and she fully committed to all functions, satellite days, meetings, and outside NA/AA meetings. My daughter's sobriety began that day. That didn't mean that everything was going to be easy and uneventful, although I hoped it would.

Setting up shots in our home was one of the best tools at my disposal in early recovery. We worked on these together, and I learned that she could manipulate her way around the shots if I made them too complicated or frivolous. The best thing I could do was to *keep it simple*. I determined what was most important, wrote it out, set tangible consequences, and enforced them. I believe that having the parent group and the staff backing me up gave me the strength to hold on to the shots and not get sidetracked. It helped keep me sane and helped my daughter have clear direction in what was expected of her. No more fighting. All I had to do was ask her to go look on the fridge instead of standing toe-to-toe in a battle of wills. It was liberating! My first shots were all about relying on the staff to make decisions for us instead of being parent-driven! I think I revised those shots at least five or six times.

My daughter took the bus and the light rail to get to her sober high school. She fell asleep on the bus and rail more than once. I remember the time that the GPS tracker I had on her (yes, I was still holding on to my codependent ideas!) showed that she was in the Houston Metro bus barn! I called them, but they had already found her and were taking her to class. It was time for me to wake up too. I shared my weaknesses in my first step study and got support and understanding from those amazing women. I shared in the meetings, at coffee, with the staff—I was ready for help.

I remember sharing in a meeting that riding the roller coaster of any high school girl was not the smartest way to parent! I like the phrase—*let go or be dragged!* Knowing it in my head and applying it only happened after I was dragged around for a while and got pretty bloody. I am always surprised when I find my hands firmly on that rope, but this program has given me a voice in my head that shouts, "Let the rope go!"

Half measures availed us nothing. I wanted her to succeed, I wanted her to benefit from the promises, I … I … I … One of the lessons I had to learn over and over—*I can't want it more than she does.* She was sober but not always as focused and committed to the work as I thought she should be.

I was making us both crazy and finally decided to listen to what my sponsor had been telling me—to just focus on my own program. I knew that trusting the process meant getting as far away from my daughter's program as I could and investing in my own. I attended three back-to-back step studies, including coleading the last one. I learned from working step 4 why I often behaved in destructive ways. I learned more about my family of origin and came to terms with my role in that family. I also connected with women who have been part of my life in good and bad times since then.

I played in the Cornerstone softball tournaments and scraped my kneecaps over first base more than once! I went to parent retreats, led topic, hosted girls, had girls' night, went to functions, began sponsoring, worked on Serenity Saturdays for the moms, and participated in three talent shows, which I absolutely loved. I grew so much because I was surrounded by healthy women. I was enjoying life and learning to breathe.

My kid had her own path, and I had mine. I began to understand the addict brain, and some slogans that helped me were, *"Time takes time," "God is everything or he is nothing," and "Let go and let God." The Serenity Prayer* has been the failsafe tool for me. It reminds me that I need to look at my part but I don't have to take care of everything.

She left our home with a stranger on the first day of her senior year—I was terrified. My head went to the worst-case scenario. I had the support of staff, kids, and parents. I remember telling my husband that if he wanted to see me he would have to be at a meeting because I couldn't go one day without one. He was there. We did not go through this alone. When I reached out, there was always an answer to my call. My family is better off by going through this program.

I asked a staff member if I should start arranging to get my daughter back into treatment, and he gave me simple advice: you're getting ahead of yourself. Wasn't that my fallback mode of operation? Hadn't I learned better than that? I realized that this program was one of *progress, not perfection.* Of course it turned out that there had been nothing to worry about.

I stayed connected with the people who showed me when I was slipping back into old behavior. I was able to change that and correct my course. I was relieved that I didn't have to be perfect for the program to work, and neither did my daughter, my husband, or anyone else in our world.

This program has strengthened my belief that I am not the higher power—that God cares about my life and the lives of those I love. It has strengthened my faith and has shown me that I can trust something other than my own capabilities.

Our lives have changed so much. The tornado has subsided. Our daughter is now twenty and in college. She lives at home, and we communicate on a real level. I am aware that I can slip into codependency, so I stay connected to those who can hold me accountable and remind me of the tools that I have learned.

God meets me where I am and provides me with what I need at the time. One day at a time—not getting ahead of myself.

Absolute Fear

My family came to Cornerstone when my then fifteen-year-old son was preparing to discharge from residential treatment after a nine-month stay. He was placed in residential treatment because of an addiction to marijuana and severe depression. At fourteen years of age he was suicidal, attempting to take his life on multiple occasions, twice at home.

While we had some form of peace while he was out of the house and in treatment, our family was broken. My son hated me. My daughter hated my son for what he was doing to the family. I had resentments toward my son for turning all of our lives upside down. The one bright spot was that my wife and I were always on the same page and our relationship was strong, perhaps even stronger than ever, as we came together to deal with this tragedy.

The weeks leading up to his discharge from residential treatment were unsettling to say the least. Those feelings and memories of our household being out of control were creeping back into my mind. Absolute fear is probably the best way to describe it. There were so many unknowns, so many unanswered questions. Would he just go back out and start using again, and would nine months and tens of thousands of dollars be wasted? How could we ever trust him again? How could we let him out of our sight? How was he going to have friends and socialize? Where would he go to school? How would he spend his free time? Was he going to live or die? Not knowing how any of this was going to turn out was eating me alive, driving me crazy.

We had done a lot of research while he was in residential treatment about what we were going to do after he came home. We were looking for the right support group for ourselves and for him. We visited several programs but did not really know what to look for, so I must admit that a big part of our decision was convenience, although it's hard to consider any of this convenient. Cornerstone and his school were close together.

For the first thirty days or so, our son reluctantly went through the motions. At first, he resented it and tried to manipulate his way out of it. He said all the Cornerstone kids were gay, always hugging each other and giving each other massages. He complained that the days were too long and hard and that he wasn't getting enough sleep. Later we came to understand that this was all part of the manipulative nature of addicts. After about thirty days, he began to develop friendships and started having fun.

Going into Cornerstone, I did not understand recovery, and I certainly did not understand the concept of parent-driven recovery. However, my personality is such that if I am going to get involved in something, I am going to do it right or I don't do it at all. The decision to get involved and do everything the Cornerstone program called for was an easy decision for me since I realized that this was a life-and-death situation and I was going to do everything I could to save my son (It wasn't until about three years later that I finally accepted that I could not save my son but that I could save myself and lead a happy life based on spirituality). So I did everything Cornerstone suggested. I read the books, went to meetings, got a sponsor, worked the steps, did three dad step studies, did wilderness trip workouts with the kids, did nighttime mountain biking with the kids in Memorial Park, did dad retreats and dad wilderness trips.

Gradually I started feeling better about myself as a parent. I felt like I was becoming a better person, kinder and more loving. We hosted Friday- and Saturday-night functions. We became a host family and had kids staying in our home the majority of the time. I learned a lot by hosting kids in our home, not only about the kids and their struggles but about myself. I learned that most of these kids are good, decent human beings who have a disease and made some bad choices. They are intelligent individuals with big hearts and a good sense of humor and adventure. I also learned that most of them have low self-esteem, and I saw how many of the Cornerstone concepts are designed to help them overcome this issue.

We got control of our house back by setting "shots." At first this was difficult, not so much the setting of the rules but coming up with consequences that : 1) were appropriate in terms of severity; 2) we could live with; and 3) we were willing and committed to following through with. We made some mistakes along the way. One of the things that helped me the most in setting and enforcing the "shots" was hosting other kids since it is a whole lot easier and less emotional to follow through on consequences when you are dealing with someone else's kid. There were several instances where the hostee would break a shot and had to move out of our house. When this occurred, we had meaningful conversations where all parties spoke and understood what had occurred and the related consequences. One of the other important things I learned through this process was that most of these kids want to be held accountable.

I've learned to overcome my fears by surrounding myself with an excellent support system and to trust God. There may be other ways to achieve this, but the only thing that has helped me achieve this so far in my life is by working the twelve steps. At first I did not understand why I should do this since I am not the addict. But now I understand. The steps made me do a lot of soul searching, brought me closer to God, and made me a better person who is now committed to helping others through service work.

A Healthy Relationship with Myself

Life was good. And then it wasn't. And then it became beautiful, beyond my imagination.

My sister and I grew up in a loving, two-parent family. I attended the best public schools and excelled in academics and athletics. I made friends easily. The first time I smoked dope, I was fifteen years old, primarily due to peer pressure. I didn't care for it much. I was liked by the jocks, the smart kids, and the stoners. I got a kick out of being the "good" kid on the diving team who was also "bad." Bottom line, I liked attention and sought it through both positive and negative actions.

At fifteen and a half, I went out joyriding and wrecked my neighbor's car. I was arrested. My parents did not rescue me. Initially the judge wanted to put me under house arrest for the summer. My mom disagreed, saying that I would have no way of making money to pay for the damages. The judge loved that, removed the house arrest requirement, and ordered me to pay $2,500 for the damages. I worked an entire summer cutting lawns every day and delivering newspapers in the morning and evening to pay for what I had done.

We moved to Wisconsin when I was sixteen, and I had my inaugural taste of hard liquor my first night there. I felt alive, self-assured, and in control when I had booze flowing through my system. Alcohol enabled me to be who I thought I wanted to be. I wasn't afraid of social situations, girls, or much of anything. I ended up drinking half a bottle of Jack Daniels and was arrested for the second time in my life.

I got the speech from my dad, "You have two strikes. You don't want a third one," and I was pretty convinced that my parents would send me to military school and I would lose all of the work I had put into my diving career if I got in trouble with the law again. I continued to get As in school and won more and more diving competitions, which fed my ego and drew the attention of college recruiters. I ended up attending Purdue University on a diving scholarship.

I went on to college and probably drank less than others because I had serious priorities. The academic and athletic competition was a great high for me. I could change the way I felt about a lot of things when I was on the diving board. I finished out my diving career and graduated with honors. I had a number of job offers.

I chose a job in Chicago and found it easy. For the first time in many years, I had plenty of free time and a pocketful of cash. Six months later I was arrested for a third time, for DUI. I lost my license for a year but still did not believe I had a drinking problem; I had a drinking and driving problem. My solution was not to drive when I was drinking.

My unabated drinking continued for twenty-three more years, following the pattern I had established earlier in life. I got into and out of trouble in a repetitive cycle. My alcoholism got progressively worse, and the cycles got shorter and more destructive as time wore on.

In 2008, my son's hockey team had made it to state for the high school ice hockey championships. We had family in town, and I threw a party the night before the finals. I drank too much and felt terrible in the morning. To take the edge off, I decided to finish the rest the rum left in a bottle that was in our pantry. A half a dozen shots or so later, I felt better and able to deal with the day. After the game I was still over the limit and panicked when a tire blew out, but the police didn't stop and I thought I had dodged disaster one more time. However, my wife noticed that the pantry bottle was now gone, and she deduced that I had finished it before leaving for the game. It was shortly thereafter that I entered an outpatient treatment program, after which I entered a twelve-step program and did well for a while.

I got a sponsor, worked the steps, and managed to stay sober for nine months. However, I never really understood the idea of "turning my life and will over to the care of God," much less "living life on life's terms." I relapsed four times in close succession.

One of the greatest lies the disease tells the afflicted is that you are only hurting yourself and that if everyone would just leave you alone and mind their own business, you would be fine. I barely noticed that my daughter was following my lead. When I witnessed my daughter at her lowest point, I could not understand why this child who seemed to have everything going for her couldn't be happy and couldn't see the beauty in her life and couldn't see the harm she was causing herself and others.

My wife and I were terrified, baffled, and hurt, and it was a moment of clarity for me. It was then that I started to realize the impact of my own alcoholism on others, especially my wife. She had lived for years wanting me to be happy and joyful and grateful for the gifts I had been given, and I could not. I had no clue how to do that. Happiness was for other people who just seemed to be luckier and more fortunate than me.

We started the Cornerstone program for our daughter. My wife and I were able to get on the same page, create a unified front, and start restoring some sanity to our home. The situation forced us to work together. We could no longer be divided. Our daughter started to get better.

However, there was still a bunch of stuff in our marriage that wasn't working, and that stuff started to come back up after the initial hurricane passed. To me it was like slamming on the brakes of a car—we prevented a major accident, but then all the crap from the backseat flew up to the front of the car and we needed to start dealing with that if we were ever going to be able to drive the car together again.

Instead of embracing real recovery, I went the other way and dove into guilt and shame and withdrawal from the family. I was resentful about having to come clean with my own drinking and accept responsibility for my part. I went back to old behavior.

On July 12 of 2011, my daughter and my wife held me accountable for drinking when our household shots clearly state that the use of drugs and alcohol in the house is prohibited with the consequence being alternative living arrangements. I moved out of the house not knowing what was going to happen. Initially, I was filled with remorse, regret, and shame.

> Q: Who gets drunk when their kid is in a recovery program?
>
> A: An alcoholic that has no true recovery under his or her belt.

I knew something in my life had to change. I had been involved in a feeble relationship with the twelve steps long enough at this point to at least know how the story was going to end if real recovery didn't occur.

I went to a meeting to pick up my fourth desire chip and to start over again. My daughter was pissed, but she attended that meeting along with a couple of Cornerstone kids we had hosted. They will never know what that meant to me—the support that only another alcoholic can provide. My daughter asked me what I was going to do differently this time. I told her that honestly I did not know. Her observation was that I was a white knuckler—trying to fight this thing as opposed to surrendering and letting other people help me. She went on to point out that while I was attending both my own twelve-step meeting and Cornerstone, I was really not participating and until I did, things wouldn't change.

I called another Cornerstone dad who was in recovery, and he became my sponsor. We did a steps 4 and 5 over the events that occurred, and I started attending morning meetings every day. He encouraged me to let go of my guilt and shame, which weren't doing me any good and certainly weren't helping my family. My way of thinking started to change. My life started to change.

I realize now that alcohol had been my shield from the difficult things in life, but it distanced me from all of the good things as well. I used it to get through uncomfortable situations, but it ended up taking control and blasting through all the good stuff. My child's addiction is what led me to sanity. I no longer struggle through every day of life, unable to enjoy anything and missing out on all the blessings and joy that were right in front of me.

I have learned the following:

- God works a great deal of his miracles through people on earth. If I am isolated and not connected to people, I miss out on the miracles.
- When we all quit trying to fix each other and started to look at our own problems, the cure started to take effect. When we extended that to trying to be of service to others—our whole lives changed.
- In many cases, the things I thought were calamities were truly blessings. They were the things that created real growth in my life. The things that I thought were important, like chasing success, didn't lead to happiness.
- Real faith came when I was finally at a point where I had to hand my daughter over to God and accept that I could not be God for her. That is when I found faith.
- If I don't like some part of myself or my life, there is either something I need to start or stop doing, something I need to learn, or something I need to change.

Today, I have a relationship with my wife and daughter that I did not think was possible. I had hoped and prayed that God would restore my family, but he did much more. He gave me a family and a life that I could not even imagine.

Today, I have a healthier relationship with myself. This has been the key. I couldn't love others in the right way because I hated myself for many, many years. I can see the goodness in me and I have purpose in life, far beyond making a paycheck.

The Beauty of Play

I cannot express the impact and value of a softball tournament in a family recovery environment. A tournament can be well organized and run smoothly, but the fellowship among teams who are celebrating health, life, and their support for each other is amazing. It feels good to look around the hundreds of people, know almost everybody, and feel the love and support each has for the others. The connection with every single one of them is amazing.

My son played select baseball. There were times he was in two select teams while playing for the city league at the same time. He played for two Youth Baseball World Series teams before he started using drugs. He was a remarkable athlete and a formidable pitcher. His father and I had many dreams of his future as a professional player. We lived in baseball parks, watched tournament after tournament for one weekend after another for many years.

Once he got involved in drugs, all those dreams vanished into thin air. I spent my weekends looking for him, waiting anxiously, or praying that we would be able to find him and that he would be alive by the end of the day. There was no more cheering on weekends but tears and fears of the unknown. I never thought I would see him happy again, much less pitching. We lived in terror for three and a half years. I wasn't expecting the recovery program's softball tournament to be such a big deal after the intensity of his years in baseball.

When we played softball with all of those other families, I saw him smiling, talking to people, clowning around, going from one group of kids to another, and pitching something close to the sport that he had loved so much!

As I saw my son playing ball with true friends and his friends' parents, wearing shorts and raggedy shoes, not dressed like the athlete I had believed he was meant to be, that is when it became really clear that I had been doing it wrong. I had been focusing on the least important things in life. Now my son has skills that I thought he would never have.

Yesterday my son was a normal fifteen-year-old hanging out with a bunch of normal teenagers and young men and women. In spite of what society might think, these are normal kids, our kids in recovery. They all looked so happy and so full of life. They cheered for their parents and for the kids who had never held a bat. They cheered the effort of the kids who couldn't catch a ball. They had a day of relief from the pain they carry over the ugliness of the past and the fights with their families. Yesterday was a day for fellowship, love, caring, support, and encouragement. There was one ref that before every game said a prayer for those lives lost at war, for the veterans, and for those addicts and alcoholics out there who still suffer. We had our own veterans in those fields. These families are also soldiers of a deep, hidden, lonely, very misunderstood war. These kids are also war heroes.

Yesterday I felt happiness I thought I would never feel again in my life. I would not trade any day, not even a second spent at a World Series, for a day like yesterday. I would not trade any major league game for yesterday's games. I wished that I could stop time and enjoy those minutes, those connections with others, those feelings a bit longer. As the day ended and I was getting ready for bed, I realized that I have those connections, that relief, and those relationships now and don't need to wish for more. Last night I caught myself singing in my head the song, "Take me out to the ball game," a song I have not sung in years … a song that meant happiness, carefree moments in life … a song I would sing from the top of my lungs without thinking I was singing out of key and the loudest I would sing it the better. I have not been able to live or feel what I felt yesterday in a while. And now I know that I can laugh and play with my son in ways that I thought were gone forever.

I Got Out of God's Way

I was eleven the first time I got high. By the time I got sober at sixteen, I had used just about every drug out there—from alcohol and marijuana to prescription drugs, cocaine, and heroin. What started as what I considered normal, casual drug use quickly became a daily regimen of use/abuse.

My bottom came after a series of several rapid-fire events. First, I was jumped in a drug-related deal that resulted in my broken jaw being wired shut for six weeks. I totaled my car two weeks after getting it, and the law finally caught up with me and I was arrested and charged with drug possession. Other aspects of my life were crumbling as well.

I knew I hit bottom when my doctor told me that I could die if I threw up while my jaw was wired shut, yet I continued to get drunk and smoke heroin, two drugs that are known to cause vomiting. It wasn't really a desire to get high anymore; it was just all that I had. Happiness to me was something that existed only in movies. I was resigned that this was my lot in life—this was the path I chose, and I had to live with it.

I didn't come to the Cornerstone Recovery program to get sober; I came to find happiness. In Cornerstone, I saw kids that were just like me. Kids that had walked my same path and been in my situation, and now they were happy—truly happy. Cornerstone was different from any other group or activity my parents tried to get me to join. I didn't fit in the church youth group and I'm not a football player, despite my mother's best efforts. It seemed for a time, I didn't fit anywhere. Cornerstone offered enthusiastic sobriety for anyone who was willing. Enthusiastic sobriety changed my life. I wanted what these kids had, and I was willing to go to any lengths to get it.

The early days and months of sobriety were difficult. I attended my first Thursday meeting on February 21, 2008, and afterward one of the "winner" kids took me to his house for the weekend. I had the best time that weekend. I laughed and felt accepted.

On Sunday, I came home to my drugs and alcohol. I retreated to my room with the intent of getting high. My first God moment happened that night when my best friend, who was in rehab for the fourth time, called me and said that he was getting clean. He, too, had attended a couple of Cornerstone meetings before going back to rehab. He said he wanted to get out of rehab and work the Cornerstone program. I decided not to get high that night.

The first thirty days were the hardest. I slept with the alcohol and drugs beside my bed. Even if I didn't use them, it was comforting just knowing they were there. I dreamed constantly about getting high.

In the early days of sobriety, my actions were far from sober-worthy. My parents presented the new rules of the house entitled "Shots and Bounds" to me. There were five basic rules: drug/alcohol free, work your program, stick with "winners," rigorous honesty, and complete respect. All of the shots carry a first-time consequence of being out of the house. As my mom was going over them, I panicked. The powerlessness overwhelmed me, and I needed to get that control back. I proceeded to cuss her out, and then I left the house. The next morning, mother woke me so that we could go to the Saturday Cornerstone meeting. I got up and cussed her out again. We fought the whole way to the meeting. Later that day, she called and told me my bags were on the front porch. I was out of the house. I will always be grateful to her for this.

Cornerstone has seasoned recovery families that serve as "host families" for kids that are out of the house. I couch-hopped for a couple of days and then found a permanent host family close to my school and work because I had to walk. I didn't feel comfortable in someone else's home, and they wouldn't let me in the house when they weren't there. There were still glimpses of happiness that encouraged me. I began to feel love and acceptance from the kids, and I still wanted what they had.

About thirty days into the program, I relapsed. I put alcohol in my mouth at work and spit it out. The intent was there even if I didn't swallow. I never told anyone because I was afraid they'd kick me out of the program. This was my second moment of clarity, and I decided to make a real down payment on my sobriety. I quit my job for fear of real relapse, worked my way back into my house, and then threw away all my drugs. I decided if I was to be happy, I was going to have to work the program, go through the steps, get a sponsor, and start learning to live a sober (not just dry) life.

My priority was to follow the advice of those who knew recovery. I did nothing but eat, sleep, and breathe recovery. I worked the strongest program I could. I went through intensive outpatient treatment where I learned to quit pretending I was something I wasn't. Fear and social anxiety began to slip away, and I became comfortable sharing emotional risks. Prayer became a first instinct, and I began reaching out to newcomers.

I had become quite comfortable with the accountability and routine of IOP, so when I was given a discharge date, I felt fear creep back in. The truth is that I had only known good sobriety within the IOP structure. I wasn't sure I knew how to live, much less thrive, without that structure.

A requirement of the graduation ceremony from IOP is to make amends to your parents. In making those amends, I felt overwhelming peace and acceptance, and I could see how far I had come from that punk kid who yelled at his mother. I realized that I had needed all of the bad experiences in my life, so I could be where I was that day. Finally, I realized that God has a plan for me.

I began to understand who I wanted to be, and mediocre wasn't an option. I had early growing pains. My sponsor explained that in IOP, I shut down some areas of my life to focus on my addiction and early recovery, and now I had to work my program into other aspects of my life.

My best friend relapsed and left the program, and another friend began cutting herself and eventually relapsed. My sponsor decided to fly to Minnesota and walk home, writing his memoir along the way, and I let myself feel lost without a sponsor. I was in a bad spot. I had the idea that I had to rely on self-accountability, which is not my strength. I started sleeping in school, resented those who had abandoned me, and was codependent with those who were abandoning themselves. I had a bad attitude at school and was faking it at Cornerstone. In both areas, I was hiding the pain from my best friends' relapse.

Finally, I pulled myself out of the hole and got a sponsor. I started working a real program again and through this new sponsor, I learned much about humility. Eventually, I began to understand that pain equals growth.

A counselor once told me that if we all fully comprehended the value of pain, we'd ask for more. Soon, I would understand the true meaning of this statement.

A young man who I sponsored had a relapse. I continued to sponsor him. He had a series of relapses. Each time, we would devise a plan of action to get him back on track; but it was like watching a train wreck in slow motion with no ability to do anything about it. I kept sponsoring him as if I had the answers and could bring him back to recovery. I wanted to succeed as a sponsor more than he wanted to be sober. I had forgotten the value of accountability. My ego kept me thinking that I could save him.

He died in car crash on April 3, 2009. He was high at the time, and the wreck was his fault. I served as a pall bearer at his funeral. His death was a wake-up call and forever changed me. I had been sponsoring a man who had no intent to remain sober, withholding the accountability that may have helped him feel enough pain to stop the insanity, and helping him feel comfortable with his relapses. I learned about boundaries and not enabling someone's destructive behaviors. I learned how to enforce accountability with love.

A Vessel of Love

After a brief yet tumultuous stint of drug and alcohol abuse, my lifestyle had proven itself a dead-end. My future seemed bleak. By the time I met my bottom, my "friends" were in prison or dead—literally and metaphorically. As was I. I woke up every day wishing I had died in my sleep. I walked in fear and couldn't face life without the numbing distance of drugs and alcohol. Hope and trust were absent, and I felt little connection to a world outside of destruction and despair.

Little did I know, the day my universe collided with the path of Cornerstone I would be set free and my world would become forever expansive, full of light and possibility. I was welcomed with unshakable smiles and unconditional love. The families of Cornerstone saw me.

They understood the darkness and knew a way out. Reluctant, but desperate, I reached for their warm hands of hope and happiness and took my first leap of faith. Unknowingly, I slowly began to shed my armor, which opened my heart for love and support that ultimately would assist in learning how to love and support myself.

Through backpacking trips, weekly meetings, private sessions, weekend functions, committee retreats, girls' hangouts, and countless late-night drives to Galveston or Kingwood, my old world dissolved, and I felt a shift so dramatic I decided I never wanted to look back. I found a new purpose, a new meaning, and a genuine happiness in connection and through love. My self-esteem was rooted in positive leadership and emotional meaning rather than superficial characteristics. Relentless accountability taught me integrity, and fearless honesty taught me unconditional love is possible. Not only did I learn how to receive others' support, I too became someone who could offer strength.

The tools I learned in Cornerstone armed me with the skills I have needed to get through the hardest of times. No longer do I need to escape into the darkness. I have witnessed greatness and strength beyond what I could have possibly imagined for myself. Every day I carry what I was taught, and I am grateful for every second of opportunity. Today is my choice, and I choose to be a vessel of love, strength, and value. I know now that I have the ability to create the life I wish to have and that anything is possible. God is with me, and I walk in the direction of life and light. Never again do I want to cower in the face of growth; I have felt death, and I owe myself this chance to live.

I Found Hope on a Mountain Bike

I am a recovered alcoholic. I say I'm recovered not because I'm cured or will ever be free from the disease that I have, but because I have recovered from the hopeless state of mind and body that I found myself in twenty-six months ago today. Admitting and accepting that I was in that place was the hardest and scariest thing I've ever done. It has also been the most rewarding.

Throughout my childhood and into my teens I felt that nothing could ever go wrong. Even though friends of mine moved away and neighboring families seemed to be falling apart, I was always under the impression that none of that would ever happen to me. I had everything a young kid needed and more.

My father lost his job shortly before I turned ten, setting into motion a train of events that stripped me of my fantasy entirely. We lost our house and moved into a small apartment. My mother tried her best to support our family of four while my dad searched for a job. I no longer fit in at school and couldn't seem to make any close friendships that lasted longer than a season. I was picked on for having less money than the rest of the kids I went to school with, and for being a chubby kid. Meanwhile, my family spiraled into endless fighting over just about everything. My dad stayed home all day drinking beer and sitting on internet chat rooms while my mom was working herself to the bone. My sister, who I then shared a room with, made fun of me with friends she brought around the house. I just wanted to be loved. I wanted to be told everything was going to work out and that I was perfectly okay just the way I was.

My parents divorced that year, and my mother filed for bankruptcy. My mom, my sister, and I moved into my grandmother's house, and I shared a room with my mom, who was nothing short of falling apart at the time. To add to the situation, my grandfather developed Alzheimer's disease and became eccentric, confusing, and even violent toward us. I became very quiet. I sought escape in isolation and video games at the time. I hated being teased about my weight, and I would gorge myself in shame. My grandfather went into a facility for Alzheimer's patients, my mom worked tirelessly, and with my sister being older, I began having a lot more time alone in an empty house before my mom got home. I would do almost anything for friendship and eventually found a group of kids nearby, and we were intrigued by mischief. The same group introduced me to the kid who would give me my first drink.

I was twelve years old when I had that first drink. From that day I never drank without the resolute intent to get drunk. I remember drinking until I vomited that first night, getting burned by a cigarette, and waking up the next morning with a hangover, 100 percent ready to do it again. I was carefree when I drank. I wasn't thinking about what was going on at home, what people thought of me, what I looked like, or anything for that matter. All was right in the world.

I mustered up the courage to try drugs for the first time the next summer. I didn't get high the first time I smoked pot, but the first time I stole cough syrup from a grocery store was exhilarating to me. I finally felt cool, I like I had a purpose. I belonged to something. I didn't know at the time just how much I belonged to it and what it was trying to do to me.

I continued through junior high school getting loaded on the weekends, getting in trouble at school for inattention, and getting by making Bs in all of my classes. In the meantime, my mom started dating a guy she met online. Within two months, they got engaged, and he bought a new house for us all to move into. Everything happened so fast and I didn't even know this man, but he had a lot of money, and he was making my mom happy, so I welcomed the change. It felt like we were finally getting back on our feet, until one morning, after living with this man for a month, he announced that the marriage was off and that we needed to leave the house immediately. I'll never forget my mother's sobs on the phone when she called to tell me. Instantly, my family precipitated back into the dark uncertainty we felt we had just begun to transcend. We moved back in with my grandma, and I spent as much time as I possibly could away from the house, drinking with my "friends."

In high school, I abandoned my lifelong passion for baseball due to all the preppy kids and pursued my other dream, to play on the drum line. This placed me around a generally more loving and accepting group of friends, and I didn't really drink or use drugs for the first two years of high school. Once most of my friends graduated however, I was right back where I was in junior high. I didn't feel a part of anything, and I was left with nothing but my low self-esteem and my raging ego that pushed everyone away. But I remembered what was always there for me before when that was all I had: drugs and alcohol.

This time, I dove headfirst into drinking and using as much and as often as I possibly could. It had been a couple of years since I had done drugs, but this time was totally different. When I got high this time, I became intent on doing it every single day for the rest of my life. I began selling weed, even at school, to support my habits. I was still a "good kid" to my mom, made great grades, took AP classes, and excelled in music. Nobody suspected anything of me, so I took full advantage of that. The summer of my junior year, I would leave our townhome for a week at a time on a bender. Anything you put in front of me, I would try. I started taking pills and mixing them with alcohol and other drugs, pilfering from every medicine cabinet of every home I entered, and stealing from my friends and family. Getting loaded, how I was going to get loaded, where and when—everything about it—dominated my thoughts. I became extremely antisocial and stuck to a group of about five friends that I drank and used with and that I felt I could easily use and manipulate to get my next fix.

I began running into trouble my senior year of high school. The first was a minor in possession, followed two months later by a theft arrest. My gold-star child image was beginning to fade as my true colors began to show. In the following months, I was constantly on lockdown and did literally nothing but go to school, work after school, and go home to get messed up in my bathroom until I blacked out. I was allowed only to see my girlfriend, who I had influenced into drinking and using, and she became my connection to the other people who supported my addiction. I was becoming physically dependent on alcohol and drugs. I stashed bottles of liquor in my closet and drugs in the back of the toilet in my bathroom. When I would get a free pass for a night or two, I would go on binges that led me to overdose several times, and I was also arrested twice more. When my mom bailed me out of jail this last time, she told me—and I'll never forget the exact words she used—if I f***ed up one more time, she wasn't going to be there anymore to help me pick up the pieces.

At this point, I had tried to quit several times. After each time I got in trouble with the law, my mom, or anyone else, I was 100 percent serious about quitting. I was *done*, every time. I bawled my eyes out countless times to those who stuck around through all of it, mainly my mom and my girlfriend. I begged for another chance. Each time this happened, the periods of sobriety became shorter and shorter. But this time I was for real. I pulled together a week of sobriety before I went on my final bender. Three days before I was to appear in court to face my charges, a urinalysis inevitably awaiting me, I snapped. I stayed up all night in my bathroom, tied off with a belt, shooting half a gram of heroin into my veins: easily enough to kill a seventeen-year-old, 140-pound kid.

By the grace of a God I didn't know at the time, I didn't die, and I wasn't put in prison. I was put on probation and sent on my merry way to college. My mom was under the impression that college would "fix" me, since I had worked so hard to earn it.

I lasted two weeks in college before I found myself in handcuffs again. I woke up the next morning, remembering what my mom told me when she bailed me out of jail, and that was it. I was utterly alone. I finally realized my condition. The absolute *last* thing I wanted to do was get high or drunk, but I *had* to. I was terrified. The only way out that my irrational brain could come up with was to pull the plug on myself. So, a handful of pills, and that would be that. I called my mom weeping letting her know what I had done, that I was sorry, and that she would never have to deal with me or my BS ever again.

After driving four hours to San Antonio, my mom and stepdad arrived in time to save me from killing myself. For the next few days, I was a zombie. I didn't want to live, I was completely emotionless, and I was in extreme physical pain from withdrawals. When the fog began to lift, the insanity of cooking a shot reentered my brain. I knew I needed help, and I finally mustered up the courage to admit it out loud. I was terrified of myself. I knew I was going to die. I wanted to be committed to inpatient treatment for at least sixty days, but my health insurance had expired literally the day before I attempted suicide. Alcoholics Anonymous was the last house on the block, so I went.

In my very first meeting, I reconnected with an old friend, who I had not seen in over six years. She was an entirely different person. She was glowing, it seemed. She told me about a program called Cornerstone.

She said it was like her family. That excited a weird feeling in me … I hadn't known what family felt like since I was ten years old. I was willing to give it a shot, and I showed up to my first meeting the following day, after polishing off my stepdad's bottle of Ativan that night. To this day, the only explanation as to why I got loaded that night after discovering so much hope in that friend is that without God and the twelve steps, I have an obsession beyond my mental control that only drugs or alcohol can satisfy. I needed "one last go" before I got sober. We alcoholics think like that. We also have lots of "last gos" before the real one.

I showed up to my first Cornerstone meeting on September 6, 2012, which is my current sobriety date. What I was met with was almost overwhelming. The love and immediate acceptance I received were comparable for me at the time to finding an endless sea of dope with no consequences attached. I jumped straight in. "Don't let me go home," I told them. I knew better than to trust myself alone. Within two days I made the firm decision for myself that I was ready to leave my entire life in college behind to get into Cornerstone's outpatient program. I was perhaps overzealous, to say the least. My mom was hesitant and completely skeptical, but after talking to several other parents in the program, I was in OP and she was in Chicago, a move that had been planned for nearly a year.

Shortly after joining outpatient, I became heavily involved with the Adventure Learning Program. I saw a good friend of mine in the group return from a mountain biking trip to Big Bend, and he returned as if he had found the fountain of youth. I saw a sparkle in his eye. I got myself on a bike shortly afterward, and although I was pretty terrible and absolutely horrified of getting hurt, I continued to show up to the Cornerstone rides. This became an extremely significant outlet of self-esteem for me while going through outpatient.

My whole life, I gave up on anything I wasn't instantly good at. But I had people around me pushing me, supporting me, helping me see for myself that I was getting better slowly, and holding me accountable to keep showing up, no matter how badly I didn't want to. I can't begin to express how grateful I am for those people today, because the first mountain biking trip I went on changed the entire course of my life. I remember looking out over the mountains and the desert of Big Bend State Park after completing one hundred miles in four days. I thought, *How the hell did I just do that?* which then led to the thought, *How the hell have I done* any *of this?* I had nearly five months of sobriety at the time—more than I ever saw myself obtaining.

I caught the bug. I continued riding every week, even after that trip was over. I was already thinking about the next one. I developed a passion for open country that I never knew previously existed. There was something out there—something undeniably powerful. I felt so small, so content, and *so* free. The fact that my brothers in recovery were alongside me out there was an incredible bonus as well.

Since that trip, I've been on six more, backpacking, rafting, mountain biking, even dog-sledding. I've seen more of this country through my involvement in Cornerstone's ALP than I ever dreamed of seeing. I've built memories that I will never forget, and most importantly, I've found an outlet of service in helping to provide the same experience to others that don't even know what they don't know, like me twenty-six months ago. This year, I did the ALP's leadership course—an intense, six-month course with no pay, long hours of self-sacrifice, and a *ton* of fun. My fellow leadership course interns will be brothers and sisters of mine for the rest of my life, after what we experienced together.

Today, I recently awakened from Cornerstone, and I live in downtown Houston with a good friend of mine (also a Cornerstone and ALP leadership course alum). I sold my car nine months ago and bought Blanca, my Cannondale mountain bike and the love of my life. I've put in easily over one thousand miles on my bike this year and plan to put in several more over the next few months. My involvement and love for Cornerstone's ALP is still a very important part of my life even after awakening, because of the gift it's given me. It's inspired me to pursue an education in environmental studies/ecology, and my hope is to use that education as an activist to preserve the world's magical open country before we mine, log, dam up, and destroy all of it. I feel extremely passionate about this because of the spiritual experience that going out into the wilderness has given me, and I want more of the world to experience what I've gained from it. It's truly incredible to try to imagine that without walking into Cornerstone twenty-six months ago, I probably wouldn't have my life, and without the ALP I wouldn't have the path I have today.

I Was Determined to Protect My Son

My college roommate told me to peek outside at this guy in the red drop-top Chevrolet Impala. It was love at first sight when he looked back over his shoulder at me. I waved as I closed the door again, and I told her, "*He is mine.*" We began dating. That was my first and only semester of college. We married several years later.

Five happy years later, I found out that I was pregnant with our first child. Two weeks later we found out that my husband had a tumor near his heart. He had Hodgkin's disease (lymphoma). After eighteen months of chemotherapy, Dwayne went back into the hospital, on Christmas Eve. He died one week later at age twenty-nine. I was twenty-seven. Our son was a year and a half old. I had lost the love of my life—the only comfort and security I had ever known—on New Year's Eve, 1979.

My early childhood had been unstable, abusive, and completely barren of love and support. I was desperate to find someone to love me and to recreate my happy marriage and married very quickly. He always smelled of pot, and we moved quickly five times in a year. We divorced as quickly as we had married. Ten years of relationships passed and each man was "the one," but when I did not land a husband, my mother called me a promiscuous whore.

I moved in with a female roommate and continued to raise my son. He was a great kid. He was responsible; I hear this a lot when boys become "the man of the house." I guarded him closely and never let him out of my sight. I rarely needed to discipline him.

I took David with me to my younger sister's home in Seattle, to get away from a four-year relationship that ended badly. I never wanted to see another man. A week later, we boarded a flight back to Houston. The man seated near us complimented me on my son's good behavior. We chatted for a bit and exchanged business cards. He was funny, and as we left the plane, we were laughing. A week later, he called and asked me to lunch. We were engaged two years later. It wasn't long before we had my second son.

Both of us were swept away and completely in love with our family. My older son was thirteen and was elated with his new brother. His dreams of family and home had finally come true.

We swore off day care, no babysitters other than grandparents. I stayed home to raise him. We grew more and more protective. We moved to a cul-de-sac, and I never allowed him to leave my sight. I was determined to protect my son—and my own heart—from harm. I would not lose the love and safety I had finally found. Life seemed perfect until he was ten years old.

When he was fourteen, I found a glass pipe in his room. I didn't know anything about drugs, and I certainly did not know the difference between a pot pipe and a crack pipe. I did not know there was such a thing as a pot pipe—I thought they were always joints. I screamed with horror and grief so deeply that I was unable to speak for a week. My world crashed. My heart broke.

The insanity had begun. We told the other parents, and they denied their children were in on it too, so we showed them the photos and videos of the kids using in their homes from our son's cell phone. We invited them all to an intervention, and they all came. We all wrote letters to our children declaring our hopes and dreams for them and asking them to make wiser decisions. They all soon banned our son from their homes. Rejected and with ever-increasing low self-esteem, our son continued to make worse decisions to abuse alcohol, marijuana, then pills, then other drugs. *Our grief increased, and insanity and denial raged on for **three more years.***

He was arrested at school for taking a Xanax and was taken to jail. Two weeks later he was arrested for stealing beer and assaulting the officer who chased him. He had felony charges in two counties. He was in big trouble. We just didn't know what to do.

Finally, out of pure desperation, my husband went into a local hospital asking for help. It was a God thing, my husband says, because the young man told him exactly what our son would do and say if he tried to admit him for treatment. We were prepared. It happened exactly as predicted, and we never saw that young man again. Our son started a six-week outpatient program that day, and in that program a girl invited him to Cornerstone. He invited us to come with him. Our family's healing had begun.

It didn't go perfectly, but he wanted sobriety. He relapsed several times. We developed and stuck to our shots, and he accepted the accountability of his peers. After three years of being in and out of our home, he was a markedly different person. He no longer used abusive language. No more holes in walls. No more graffiti on the walls. Honesty and respect was natural for him now.

By working hard at our own character defects, by detaching with unconditional love and allowing our son the dignity of falling all by himself and picking himself up again, we believe that through the grace of God, he has saved his own life.

I have now dealt with the issues of abandonment, insecurity, loss, grief, fear, and control that stemmed from my childhood. I realize that I have allowed my past to foster resentments that I felt as an adult. I let go of those resentments and am no longer a victim. I made amends to anyone I could reach who I have harmed or resented through my life. I feel the ultimate and unconditional love and worthiness that is mine. I know what healthy relationships look like. I know how to set boundaries and keep them with love.

Most importantly, I know how to unconditionally love others for who they are ... right where they are. I have accepted that I am powerless against what other people do and say, but that I must continually look within to bring change that I desire in any situation. I know to turn to God for peace and love whenever I expect that it should come from other sources. I accept life right now, not as I would have it but as it is.

I am grateful for the counselors who have worked with our family through these last three years who have given new breath to so many lives and relationships, and to others who have served as volunteers and sponsors. I finally broke my habit of codependency through awareness, and with the help of others I realize that my ego was in the way of my recovery.

I Gave Her Most Everything She Wanted

I was a very tall, very skinny, and very self-conscious kid. I was afraid of everything that attracted attention. My dad was a binge drinker. My mom's dad had died from cirrhosis of the liver from excessive alcohol abuse, and she consequently hated alcohol. She was dedicated to controlling my dad.

I loved to play in the woods behind my house, where I could spend hours in isolation. Fishing, hiking, building tree houses, and biking were all things that took me away from my home to a fantasy world, where I would not have to deal with reality. In high school I discovered basketball, and eligibility to play was the only thing that motivated me to study. I never drank in high school, for fear that I would get kicked out of basketball.

Once I graduated things changed. I had never thought about college. All of my friends were going off to school or had plans for their lives. I felt really scared and lost, with no plans for the future. I kept playing sports and worked, but then I started drinking. It was wonderful. It was a whole new world. I lost all of my inhibitions, and I turned into the life of the party. My first big drunk was scary. I drank some of my dad's liquor and blacked out while driving my car. I picked up a hitch hiker and let him drive while I became sick. Even this did not slow me down. I loved the euphoria and the freedom from feeling scared of everything.

I lived at home with my parents and went through a different job every few months. I was constantly getting into trouble for drunk driving, theft, and pretty much anything for a thrill. Sometimes I would not show up for work, and sometimes I would just quit for a better job. I had a Harley Davidson motorcycle and rode with a bunch of other bikers, but everything revolved around drinking. I was completely out of control. I got drafted into the army when I was twenty years old, which really escalated my drinking. I was an MP, and when not working we were drinking. After a year in Vietnam I was discharged and picked up right where I left off before the army.

I had been in trouble so many times without consequences I felt like I was living a charmed life. No one seemed to care about me. I was let go numerous times while driving drunk, or with no license, or for lots of illegal acts. I used the GI bill to go to school at Southern Illinois University, which was pretty much one big party to me, and I eventually flunked out. I still did not think of myself as being abnormal about my drinking as all my friends were the same as me.

I met a girl, and we eventually got married. We partied together, and I assumed this would continue through our marriage. We had two children, and I continued my drinking. My wife quit drinking, but I kept on, hiding a lot of it. We didn't get along at the end of our marriage, but I was sure it was all her fault. I had a good job and had finally finished college by going to night school. I thought that providing for my family was what marriage was all about.

I recognized that I needed to stop or control my drinking, but I could not. I had no spiritual life and was not sure if a higher power even existed. I thought that people who believed in God were weak and needed a crutch to lean on. I would quit drinking for a week or so, but then it would all come back again.

After fourteen years of my binge drinking through our marriage, my wife wanted a divorce. I thought that going into a treatment center would change her mind. I knew nothing about recovery and thought I could just learn to drink responsibly. Like I had done my whole life, I tried to manipulate and control things. At the treatment center I learned the basics to the twelve steps. I met some people there who had real drug and alcohol problems, much worse than mine (or so I thought). When I left the treatment center, my wife still divorced me, which was a surprise. I started going to meetings, hoping things could still be worked out. After a while I slowly started to realize how crazy I really was. It was embarrassing and shameful to see how self-centered and difficult I had been during my drinking days. The longer I stayed in the program and away from my alcoholic friends, the more recovery started to make sense. I realized how unmanageable my life had been. It was really weird talking about a higher power, after having made fun of people who believed in God.

There were times when I wanted to drink, but there always seemed to be someone or something that would interfere with my plans. It was at a meeting that I met my present wife. We immediately hit it off and were married a year after we met. Four years later we had a baby daughter. We both thought that being in recovery and living a sober life would keep our children from making the same mistakes we had made.

Our new baby was my pride and joy. I gave her most everything she wanted, not wanting her to have a childhood like mine. Around fourteen years old she started to behave badly. We attributed that to being an adolescent and something she would grow out of. At sixteen we found out she had been drinking and sneaking out of the house at night. We immediately took her to a meeting, where she met several girls who were sober and who invited our daughter to go to meetings with them. This is where we were first introduced to Cornerstone.

I was scared to death for my daughter when I went to the first meeting. Afterward I talked to parents, and was terrified by their stories. At the time I was sick of the turmoil in our house and her craziness. I was ready to try anything. I didn't think she was as bad as the other kids in the program, but that was just me not wanting to fully see her problem. The first month or so at Cornerstone I stayed in the background, watching and learning, still afraid of the program. I slowly started to embrace it, though, and followed all of the suggestions.

The biggest thing Cornerstone gave me was hope. I saw other kids work the program and saw parents having fun with their children. Three and a half years later Cornerstone has given me back our daughter. Cornerstone has taught me how be a better parent. I learned to love my daughter without accepting wrong behavior. I learned to allow my daughter to suffer consequences for her actions and resist the urge to save her.

Today I have God to help me through the times when I think I have all the answers. I cannot say enough for all of the wonderful parents I have met at Cornerstone—people you could call at all hours and ask for advice or encouragement. I learned from the kids, from the parents, and from the staff as I came to respect and grow close to all of them. I cannot say how grateful I am to have my life and my family back.

I Walked Taller, Held My Head Higher

Insidious is defined as having a gradual and cumulative effect, like rot. Or termites. Or cancer. Or drug addiction. It was the latter—drug addiction—that my wife and I faced a little over three years ago. Our daughter was always a difficult child, and I think that this partially masked the problem.

But as all such problems go, there were signs and slip-ups, which we missed. We should have known better. We should have been stricter with her. I had experience with drugs—that is, busting people who used them when I was in the service. So I should have known better. It was our fault, as you well know, and we were failures as parents. And when we became aware of her addiction, we tried all kinds of things. I screwed her screens in to keep her—or so I thought—in at night. I just ended up with screens to repair. We tried all kinds of disciplinary schemes. Nothing would work.

My wife, bless her heart, found this group called Cornerstone. I missed her first meeting, as I was only very slightly in denial. Only very slightly, like being only very slightly pregnant. I also was without a clue as to what to do, which probably fueled my denial as well. Oh, well, I did know what to do but was afraid to. I could have turned her over to the police, but I didn't trust them, and in my heart, I knew that that wouldn't really work.

So I broke down, and when my wife went to her second meeting, I went with her. I don't remember why. I guess I wanted to support her or maybe I was just curious.

My first impression was: the room was small, the fluorescent lights were bright, and the night was dark, and we sat in a circle. There were about twenty people there, which surprised me. So many. We read this list, listened to someone speak, shared our experiences, and said a prayer at the end. What struck me the most about the meetings was that the others kept quiet and listened to the person sharing. Nobody interrupted or otherwise interfered with what the person had to say, not even after the meeting. It gave me the courage to speak too. They hugged each other. I came from a family that really didn't hug that much.

It was even worse when we went to the Houston meeting on a Tuesday night. There were fifty or more people there, which was truly intimidating. The room was big, the lights bright, and the night was dark, just like in Kingwood. There was a big bunch of old-timers, who spoke with such confidence. I don't know why, but I was intimidated by it. In spite of it, or because of it, I stuck with it. The message began its work on me.

I started sharing more. Just opening up and talking was exciting and rewarding when they all said, "Love you, George."

I read *Recovering Our Children* and *Beyond the Yellow Brick Road.* The first sentence in *Recovering Our Children* was: "It is not your fault." That sentence granted me freedom and is one that I will never forget.

Slowly, things began to make sense. The sharing helped me a lot. It forced me to organize my thoughts and to think about the meeting's topic. Slowly I learned the principles of the recovery program.

We made our rules and consequences. In order to live in our home, she had to be sober. This initially had little impression on my daughter, as she was still using. It came to a head, and we asked her to leave.

It wasn't the first time she left the house, but this time she went to live with a Cornerstone family. I will never forget that night when she left. It was after the Houston meeting. My daughter was angry. It was another dark night, and I remember standing on the porch outside the church, watching her storm off with a couple of kids.

That was the beginning of her recovery. Letting her go was not easy, but I heard in our first meeting with her counselor that we had to "trust the process." So I did. It was blind faith. I had no other alternative. My wife was scared, and I was scared and also relieved. The host family was good. They did what we were unable to do.

It was the beginning of mine, too. With her out of the house, I could begin to look to myself. The addict that was the center of the vortex was out of the way and safe for the moment.

I got a sponsor in late October of that year. At Christmas time, when I was on vacation, he told me to go to four AA meetings before the New Year. I panicked. Where was an AA meeting to be found? It was easy. I was astounded by the number of meetings that were held in Kingwood. Kingwood had at least seven meetings a day. They were grim affairs and in many ways scarier than my first Cornerstone meetings. The old-timers talked about their sobriety and all that, but what really got me was this one young kid, who was about the same age as my daughter. All he wanted to do was escape from the alcoholic trap. He wanted to wake up not feeling sick. He just wanted to wake up feeling normal. It was a cry that he was powerless over his addiction. I will never forget the pain and anguish in his voice.

Our daughter entered intensive outpatient treatment at Cornerstone while she was still out of our house. We gave her the money to get a bus ticket, and she learned to ride the bus to Houston and transfer to the trolley car and make her way from Spring Valley to Cornerstone and back. I believe that this was a very important step in her recovery.

She had to depend on herself, and she found that she could do things without our intervention. She needed to learn how to take care of herself. I started my first step study downtown with a group of Cornerstone dads. One of the dads leading it gave me a bookmark with "The Promises" on it. It started "If we are painstaking about this phase of our development, we will be amazed before we are halfway through." It promised freedom, happiness, serenity, peace, and the abolition of self-pity, self-seeking, and much more. I have a copy of it on my desk at home where I can see it when I wish. My heart lifts when I read it. It was the fourth thing that I learned that pushed me forward. I keep a copy on it by my desk in the office.

The first, as I related before, was it wasn't my fault, the second was "trust the process," the third was that boy at the AA meeting, and the fourth was "The Promises."

I kept up a steady pace of going to meetings. I went to Kingwood, Houston, The Woodlands, and All-City for almost a year. The one thing I knew was that if I slacked off and skipped a meeting, I would be done for. I would be sunk. So, I rarely, if ever, skipped a meeting. I drove myself to keep up the pace. It helped me.

The ascent wasn't always up. I fell repeatedly, but I tried to learn from my mistakes. The principle "progress not perfection" was a net that caught me when I fell. It kept me from becoming discouraged and stopping.

My step-work was a challenge. The first three steps were easy for me, but it took me nearly a year to do step four. It's painful to root around in one's soul, and I was averse to pain. Successfully completing it gave the courage to keep going.

Our daughter graduated from high school in 2007, a year after her twin sister. But she finished and did a fine job, too. Her true self finally was making itself known. We went to see her graduate. Her recovery spurred mine. I didn't want to be beaten by my daughter.

She went on the Cornerstone Wilderness Trip. We went to Palmer Church to see her be blessed by the priest.

When she returned from Wilderness Trip, I remember that I arrived at the airport a little late. I hate being late. I didn't find her right away, which only heightened my tension. I was looking for her when I heard her voice and turned to see her running at me—full tilt. She hit me at full speed, almost knocking me over. I have seldom felt as good in my life as when she hugged me. My real daughter was shining through.

My best moment was when I finished step 9, where I made amends to persons I had harmed. I walked taller, I held my head higher, and my self-esteem shot up. Step 9 wasn't easy, but after having completed step 4, I knew I could do it.

I mentioned Palmer. I was brought up that going to church was something one did on Sunday, but it never really appealed to me. I stopped when I went off to college. That was in 1972. In 2007, that changed. The Wilderness Trip blessing took hold of me and shook my soul like no other church has ever done. When the opportunity arose, I took confirmation classes and was confirmed as an Episcopalian in November. I was back in touch with my higher power. I cannot see how it would have happened without Cornerstone.

I read *The Greatest Miracle in the World*, which I would recommend to anyone. In the back, there is "The God Memo." Jessica had to read this one hundred nights in a row as a commitment for her treatment, and she can no doubt recite it. I've read it several times, not as many as the kids, but enough to understand the four laws:

- Count your blessings.
- Proclaim your rarity.
- Go the extra mile.
- Use your power of choice wisely.

So this is my journey, and this is what I've found on the way and the milestones that I've passed:

1. It wasn't my fault.
2. "Trust the process" and have the courage to stand firm with my daughter.
3. The boy at the AA meeting and his agony.
4. "The Promises"
5. Steps 4 and 9
6. My reawakening faith
7. The God memo

I still have a long way to go, but so far, it's been good.

That's my story, and I'm stickin' to it.

I Avoided Admitting Even to Myself

My entry into recovery was born out of desperation. I didn't start out to change my life. I wanted to change my step-child's life. Now nearly four years later, I cannot imagine any other way of living. As I've been thinking lately, it's like reading a spell-binding novel; you can't get enough, you can't wait to get to the next page, the next chapter. But I'm getting ahead of myself.

I come from a practicing alcoholic/workaholic father and codependent/caretaker mother; both of my grandfathers were alcoholics, one practicing and one sober. I have four siblings, and I am the middle child. We were poor and lived in a tiny house and scraped to get by. But despite all this, my father always had money for whiskey and partying and was almost never at home. Home was not fun. Mom was seething inside but gritted her teeth and played both mom and dad. She made sure we knew all the sacrifices she was making for her kids. As a result,

I didn't have either a real mom or a real dad and didn't understand love at all. I spent my entire life trying to be sure that I wasn't like either of them, but in the process I never developed into my own "me." I became the "not them" instead. I went so far as to avoid even their many good qualities because I didn't want to be anything like them. And for this I carried heavy guilt and shame.

I cannot remember a time when I did not believe in God. We were churchgoing, praying, solid Methodist stock, and I never questioned my faith. It has occurred to me that we were more church-centric than God-centric. God's role in my life was never quite clear in my early years; even though we kept praying hard, bad stuff kept happening. Nobody could tell me why, so I think eventually I decided it must be me. I didn't like being that person, so as soon as I could I took off to become someone else, someone who could be loved and who didn't have to be ashamed.

I mentioned that I am a step-parent. I came into this family five years before we discovered the drug use of our youngest child, my step-son. Those five years were certainly not without their ups and downs, but the introduction of drugs into the family ramped up the stress in our household. When we married, I was only a couple of years removed from burying my previous spouse after a long, excruciating illness. None of us really knew what we were getting into; but we did love each other.

We should have seen the drugs coming, but we didn't, or at least I didn't. All the signs were there; changing friends a lot, new friends who avoided eye contact, complete change in interests, hours and hours spent alone. We so badly wanted this child to have friends, have fun, and enjoy high school that we dropped all of our boundaries. The more we gave, the more he took. We were caught in a family death spiral, and it was ugly and loud. We did insane things to try to turn it around, but it just got worse. Fortunate for us all, my wife reached out and found Cornerstone.

I began the recovery journey in a state of fear, uncertainty, denial, and naiveté. I didn't understand where we were, I didn't understand where we were headed, and I sure didn't know how to get there. I struggled with my part in the dynamic more than my wife or child did.

Being a step-parent, I was trying to "cherry pick" which family issues I wanted to deal with, and I would let my wife handle the tough ones.

For a few months, I went through the motions, got superficially involved, acting the part, talking the talk. But once I started to dig a little, I started to experience discomfort with thinking of this as "their problem." I was feeling dishonest and irresponsible, and I was sinking into depression. I was anxious and angry, pompous and prideful, impatient and controlling.

I realized that I had not been carrying my weight in the healing process, and if we were to survive as a family, I had to be entirely involved with recovery. So I started working my program, tentatively at first, building momentum as I progressed.

My first year was full of activities, parent retreats, functions, groups, and meetings twice a week. I was going through all the motions. I got a sponsor, started working the steps, and went through a step study. I was pretty superficial in my work with my sponsor. Looking back on it, I was still trying to fix my child and leave myself out of it. I was afraid of the rigorous honesty required to progress, because it would force me to reveal my unlovable, unworthy, real self.

Over the second year I really worked hard on another round of step study. I was thorough, but that was my way of covering up my lack of going deep. I did bond with the other men in the step study, though, which prepared me for my later work on the real issues.

At the previous year's parents' retreat, it was recommended that we each read *The Greatest Miracle in the World* and focus on the chapter called "Memo from God." At the time my child was reading of the "God Memo" as part of a hundred-day commitment. I thought it might help our relationship for me to do the same. I made it through about forty days, but I was working with my head instead of my heart, and lost interest. I could tell that I still was not totally committed.

I kept meeting with my sponsor and actually worked pretty hard on steps 1 through 4, but I could not get myself past 4. I rationalized that I wanted it to be perfect before I moved on. Well it never got perfect, and I never moved on. In fact, I kept recycling through step 4, kept feeling worse about myself, and became convinced that really I was unlovable and unworthy. At this point I screwed myself right into the ground, and my chronic depression kicked in bigger than ever.

In my third Cornerstone year, our family from the outside looked like a poster family for Cornerstone. My child was doing well, and my spouse took a second step study and then co-led a third step study. I co-led a step study and was proud of myself, looking experienced and wise to all the "rookies."

I finally got around to reading *The Shack*; I loved the book, but it struck me that in the end Mack was everything I was not. The rest of my family was doing great, making progress, being "real," and embracing recovery. I was not, and it further convinced me of my weakness. Depression hit me like a bus, and I sunk deeper than I ever had before. Thank God that I admitted to my spouse that I was having thoughts of suicide, and at that point things kicked into high gear.

With a strong shove from my wife, I got going on two fronts. The first was to meet with my favorite clergyman, and the other was to reach out to my Cornerstone family for a new sponsor. I had hit bottom, I knew I couldn't do this myself, and I asked God for help, and he really came through for me.

I had an incredible experience meeting for fourteen weeks with seven others and my clergyman focusing on "family-of-origin" issues. The honesty was stunning, and we all held each other accountable for being real. I dug into areas of my life that I had avoided admitting even to myself, much less other people. It became clear to me that I was the member of my family with the more serious disability, not my child. As the weeks passed, I could feel my depression lift and my anger subside, and rigorous honesty become possible.

I started weekly meetings with a new sponsor, who was an absolute godsend. He really saved my life, or at least my marriage and my recovery. He gave me his time, his patience, his wisdom, his insight, his calm understanding. He became my spiritual teacher, made me feel loved, made me dig deep, helped me understand that I could be flawed and still be loved, taught me to cut some slack to myself and others, and got me through the twelve steps. He keeps me honest, probes for soft spots, bounces back weak answers, and doesn't judge me or preach to me. God knew just what I needed.

In step 9, I made amends to my spouse, my four kids, my deceased spouse, my deceased parents, and others. My nightly step 10 journal keeps me in touch with my recovery and my defects. Step 11 keeps me grounded in God and his will in my life. Through this work, my priorities were starting to get in order; I was feeling less anxiety, less depression, and less stress.

In my fourth Cornerstone year, I continued weekly meetings with my small group at church, and it became a more significant source of support for me. Continuing with my sponsor, I became more rigorous about studying, journaling, and praying, trying to maintain the momentum I had built the previous year.

At about midyear, I began to get involved with Al-Anon, visiting different groups and meetings to find the one that felt right. I was looking for a group that keep me excited about recovery, would hold me accountable for continuing my work on steps 10 through 12, and would give me opportunities for service to other Al-Anons. Compared to Cornerstone, I found a big difference in the feeling of love and support at Al-Anon, but it was time for me to launch this thing and see if it could fly. I couldn't stay in Cornerstone forever.

Of course, I am a recovering compulsive and am still a work in progress, and I guess always will be. I have found a comfortable rhythm for my life revolving around maintaining my serenity, keeping my side clean, and staying out of other people's stuff. I am feeling good about my instincts, and I can let others (especially my child) set their own direction and priorities without interfering or worrying. I have far better (but still a long way to go) insight into my defects and how I used to let them cripple me before my Cornerstone experience.

I have found three Al-Anon meetings that are each very different, but each is important to me so I can't bring myself to drop any of them. It's not the same feeling as Cornerstone, but I'm ready for it.

As I stated before, I now cannot imagine any other way of living. I can't get enough; I can't wait to get to the next page and the next chapter. Whatever comes next, I have found serenity, and I'm going to work to keep it.

I Have Met the Devil

It turns out that not everyone grows up with heavy-drinking parents in a heavy-drinking neighborhood with a heavy-drinking extended family. Not every dad insists you taste the wine. Not every priest lets eleven-year-old girls finish off the communion wine. Not every gang plays basement Ping-Pong where the winner chugs a whiskey sour. Not every family has multiple suicidal cousins. But I didn't know that.

I became the fixer. Me and Harvey Keitel. I either created distractions or mediated frequent family arguments. I excelled so the family looked good. I helped my anxiety-prone sister with a social life, always be cheerful, avoiding the loudest scenes. I left home at seventeen and stayed gone for years at a time. And I love them all.

In college I liked drinking and smoking dope; neither became a problem for me. I still enjoy wine with supper, but now I keep looking over my shoulder for that cunning and powerful demon.

Marriage at nineteen was one of the few smart things I did as a teenager. Love does not protect you from the weirdness, but it certainly gives you an edge. We're celebrating forty years this month. His family is as nutty as mine with addiction, mental illness, and young deaths. His sister and brother-in-law entered the recovery world decades ago and are rocks of recovery. I owe them.

After my mother's young death (cirrhosis), we decided to have a kid. The light of my life, he easily excelled at academics, sports, art, conversation, everything. People loved him. He won awards, trophies, and contests. He was funny. Perfect. I cherish memories of reading to him and singing him to sleep. Holidays were calm. Arguments were civilized. We ate dinner together every night. We went to all of each other's events. We hugged. We talked openly about the dangers of drugs. We were clear about principled behaviors and held each other accountable. All of us would walk around saying, "We are the happiest family we know." Seriously.

"Parents: the antidrug" is bullshit. This smart kid was as aware as anyone of the risks of drugs and his personal genetic super-danger. At fifteen, he was an addict two minutes after an emergency room morphine injection. The demon had him, but we were not clued in. He started doing DXM and Xanax. The demon got stronger. Problems with teachers, progressively bad grades, little lies that became big lies, cheating, missing jewelry, car wrecks, vandalism, withdrawn behaviors, weird friends ... all rationalized at the price of chronic insomnia.

When my husband wanted to deal with the obvious problems, I started blaming *him* for being paranoid and overly sensitive. We went from incredibly intimate best friends to crazy antagonists. I began to create distractions and got in the middle of every family argument. I started really excelling at work on time-consuming projects. I found ways to hide my son's increasingly bizarre behavior from the outside world. Flash backs to my childhood kept showing up in my midnight cry fests.

Xanax is vicious. There was no hiding from my son's rages. His downward spiral intensified and the family counselor was no help. The kid went from an elite athlete to a mugshot. We put a lock on our bedroom door for our own protection. Fights; police; scary people; car wrecks; violence; embarrassing events; punched walls; late night suspicious activity ...

Still trying to be normal, I was "helping" the senior with homework, giving him money for "dates," talking to teachers on his behalf, never counting money in my wallet so I wouldn't notice if some was missing. I lied for him. Social situations were avoided. I was sick all the time— physically, mentally, and emotionally. I put on weight. I have never been so sad in my entire life.

I have met the devil. It stole my son. It stole my husband. It stole me.

Then a whisper told me to get a grip. The whisper said, "You can't control anything else, but you *can* lose some weight." I joined Weight Watchers, met some people, lost twenty pounds, and started thinking a bit more positively. That baby step toward sanity allowed me to hear my husband when he withstood some horrible words from me to force me to see reality. I cried for two days and got the boy into rehab in Houston. It saved his life and created a huge rift between us. I joined Cornerstone.

Wow—what a cult! That first, "Hi, Janet" almost pushed me out of the room. The cheerfulness was obviously fake. The hugs were awkward. I honestly hated almost everything about Cornerstone. But I had nowhere else to go. This was it, and *it* really sucked. I quietly cried a lot, reciting the Serenity Prayer every five minutes. Without talking to anyone, strangers kept hugging me. It was like being water boarded. I kept coming back.

Then there was a meeting where the topic was resentment. I was able to come up with a zillion resentments in my first sobbing sharing. I went home and started writing; resentments poured out like lancing a boil, giving palpable relief and my first tiny glimmer of hope in years. I kept coming back.

My son got out of rehab after thirty days full of incredible resentment toward me. It was entirely my fault, of course. He spent five minutes in a Cornerstone counselor's company and then walked. He did quit Xanax; opiates became his new drug of choice. At least the rages were gone; he just became a ghost. He basically divorced himself from us, showing up every week or so to let us know he was alive and to be mean. I kept coming back.

Rustling up some humility, I got a sponsor and began step work. Acceptance wasn't hard; that resentment topic had turned on the lights. The three Cs were made more than clear to me. But it turns out that every step that involved God *was* hard for me. It wasn't until I realized that I was intimate with the devil that I also realized that there had to be a higher power. I am glad to have found a spiritual path that works for me. Meditation and prayer are now part of my waking routine. This is a big gift of my recovery. I kept coming back.

My son was out of the house for months and finally returned when he agreed to attend ninety meetings in thirty days. I do believe he tried to quit using. It got better for a while. Of course, he relapsed. Things started going downhill, and we were about to kick him out again, albeit with a lot less personal angst and no anger. I loved him and was sad but was not ready to destroy the life I had started rebuilding.

To our total shock, he chose detox. Five days later he got out, convinced he did not need any more treatment. The next day I found three guitars missing. The kid got a choice: residential treatment or residential jail. It took a few days, but I finally flew with him to the desert and admitted him to a one-year program the day before his twentieth birthday. He was high on LSD, opiates, and DXM. Not a fun trip.

I believe in guardian angels now. My son was my mother-in-law's favorite grandson. She had been devastated—one more grandchild grabbed by the demon. She died the week after he went into the program. Residential treatment is not cheap, but we instantly inherited enough money to pay for the first three months. My husband's total inheritance eventually covered most of the costs. More significantly, her death was the first thing that got through to our son after he detoxed—grief was his first emotion in years. Not fun, but a breakthrough. I am grateful for my mother-in-law in more ways than I can ever count. Recovery is rarely a straight path. Her spirit played a huge role in his second (sigh) residential program too.

My son's arrogance, intelligence, talents, charm, and manipulation skills make him a tough case. He walked several times. Thanks to Cornerstone's parent training, we do not enable him in relapse, and we support but do not disempower him in recovery. Today he is sober, working, going to college, meets with his sponsor, and loves the recovery community. We talk every few days. Words of love, gratitude, and hope abound.

My son has a future because we learned how to safely love an addict and how to motivate him to seek recovery. I worked my steps—hard. Our whole family has embraced recovery. We learned all we could about this disease. I frequently recommend Twersky's book, *Addictive Thinking*. I have a spiritual life that sustains me. I am now in touch with emotions that had been buried below decades of denial and codependence. I am a regular at Nar-Anon meetings and give back whenever I can.

Keep coming back.

Expect miracles.

Love always wins.

Addendum

What Is Treatment?

There are times when in the midst of a crisis a parent will decide to move his or her child to a new school, a new church, a new treatment program, or a new city. The problem of addiction and alcoholism does not lend itself to a geographic solution. Who are the easiest kids to make friends with? The drug users.

Once it has become clear that our child has a problem, we start looking for a solution. Most parents start by contacting anyone they know in a helping or medical position. Ultimately the word *treatment* will come up. This refers to a clinical course of therapy from a licensed professional. Most families with a substance-abusing teen will ultimately need treatment. Some do not. Matching the treatment to the family is very important. If your teen is in imminent danger (is suicidal or has overdosed), you need a hospital with a medical staff and 24–7 availability of care. If you do not need a hospital to keep your child alive, find an Alternative Peer Group (APG), get started as a parent or parents, and get your teen there with the guidance of the APG staff. Most families go through several years of trying one therapist after another before finding a solution that works. If you begin with the APG, you will soon be directed toward the professional help that is needed as an adjunct to the programming offered by the APG.

The parents' involvement in the recovery process is essential regardless of the type of treatment the adolescent receives. If you are committed to do your best, to go to any length to encourage and support your child's recovery from addiction, then you are willing to actively participate in your own change process along with your child. If your child is already in treatment, it is best that you find an APG and get involved. The APG is the best possible adjunct to any outpatient care and is the most effective aftercare to residential treatment.

Most states have strict insurance guidelines that determine the treatment that will be covered by insurance depending on the presenting problems. Another source for information on the diagnostic criteria for various levels of treatment is the American Society of Addiction Medicine's "Patient Placement Criteria" manual. There are a number of levels of care for treatment:

- Inpatient
- Wilderness treatment
- Residential
- Intensive outpatient
- Supportive outpatient
- Group counseling
- Individual counseling
- Family counseling
- Case management

There are several conventional schools of thought about selecting a starting point for treatments. One is to start with the most restrictive (in a hospital) and ease up as the client demonstrates the ability to function within any given level. This is the fastest way to start, but there are reasons that this might be counterproductive. The other is to start with the least restrictive and up the level as the client demonstrates the inability to function at that level. It takes more time, and bad things can happen if you require the teen to relapse over and over to show you what level of treatment he needs.

Inpatient, wilderness, and residential treatments are focused on getting the teen under control, with a relatively small amount of time spent on the environment to which the teen will return. All remaining levels of care have to prioritize the teen's environment, including family and peers.

If the teen is highly resistant and has no intent to get or stay sober, forcing the teen into residential treatment may be a waste of money and more importantly may sour your child on the possibility that treatment can be a solution. Nevertheless, you cannot afford to take the risk of allowing self-destructive behavior to continue. If this is the case, begin by participating as a parent in an APG. Develop and use your rules and consequences along with the united front to help reduce the teen's resistance. If this fails, you can escort your teen to a residential or wilderness facility. A minor can be admitted against his or her will in most adolescent facilities.

The danger of the adolescent's behavior is a factor. If the child is engaged in extremely dangerous behavior, start with the most restrictive treatment and introduce more freedom as the danger remits. If the child's behavior is minimally dangerous, the least-restrictive approach coupled with parental involvement in the parent program of an APG will give the teen an opportunity to discover the insanity of drug use. In any case, you will not be entirely successful unless you participate in your own process of change by using the tools in this book.

Another factor is the family's and the adolescent's readiness for change. An addict who is not interested, doesn't see the need, and is perfectly content with life is not a great candidate for treatment but will likely become so if the family is ready and willing to take a hard stand and allow the teen to feel the hard consequences of drug use. Again, that parents' involvement in an APG will be of great help.

If everyone including the addict is ready, willing, humble, and eager, the least-restrictive approach will work.

Inpatient Treatment

Patients who require twenty-four-hour monitoring by physicians due to overdosing, alcohol poisoning, and suicide attempts are treated in a hospital setting. Patients typically stay for three to ten days in a hospital before being transferred to residential treatment. The hospital setting is conducive to medical care, is not designed as a long-term residence, and is much more expensive than residential treatment so most insurance carriers will encourage a transfer to residential treatment and limit inpatient treatment days. If your child overdoses, is acutely intoxicated, or is suicidal, inpatient care is warranted. Once the teen is has detoxified and is no longer suicidal, a transfer to residential treatment is recommended.

Wilderness Treatment

Wilderness treatment programs are designed to provide an intense group experience for the adolescent who is highly resistant and/or highly entitled. In small groups, patients in the program set out from a base camp with guides and counselors to experience several weeks or more of rugged, no-trace camping and trekking. Wilderness programs are typically in mountainous areas, although some operate in desert areas.

Residential Treatment

Residential treatment facilities provide room and board for all of their patients, who typically remain in the facility for thirty to ninety days of treatment. The activities vary and include group therapy, twelve-step meetings, school, outdoor activities, individual counseling, psychiatric consultation, and family engagement on a regular basis. The facility will have a dining hall, dormitories or semiprivate rooms, usually a gym, and comfortable outdoor spaces. The patient's length of stay in a residential setting is usually determined by an insurance carrier. Research on the success of patients after discharge indicates that ninety days is optimal, although rarely approved for payment.

If residential treatment is warranted for your child, do not wait until after graduation or after his birthday or after your niece's wedding or after the holidays. Do it now. All of those events will only be miserable if he is acting out through them. I have seen many kids spend Christmas, their birthdays, and other important moments in rehab. What a powerful message. One is not entitled to experience these normal things while self-destructing.

Find a residential program that will be able to admit your child, and get him there. If your child is a minor, he or she can be admitted involuntarily. If you are concerned that he will run away if he knows that you are following through on this consequence, do not tell him until you are walking out the door to go there. If he has a friend who is supportive of his getting help, have the friend ride there with you. Last resort, you can hire off-duty policemen or police-women who will pick up your child early in the morning and escort him there.

After he's been there a week, do not rescue him when he tells you that the place is starving him, everyone is gay, they treat him horribly, they are bullying him, or any of a myriad of aces that your kids has up his sleeve to try and break you into compliance with his disease. In almost every case, after the child has been in treatment for sixty days, he usually loves it and does not want to leave. He feels good for the first time in a long time.

When being discharged from residential treatment, most teens are sure that this problem is licked. Sadly, 85 percent of patients completing a residential treatment program relapse within two months of being discharged. They may be genuinely resolved to stay sober, but teens find that it is harder than they could expect. *Aftercare planning is critical.* With a six- to twelve-month (at least) aftercare plan, long-term recovery is frequently the outcome.

Almost anyone can get sober while in a residential setting, watched and supported 24–7. Most residential programs help develop an aftercare plan for the teen before completing the discharge, but very often the parents and teen are so thrilled at the turn-around that they blow it off. Some of the aftercare plans developed in treatment facilities are not realistic. They may select which former friends with whom your child should reunite. These friends are usually pretty squeaky clean and do not have the skills to hold your child to his or her commitments. They may suggest that you send your child back to the same school, justifying that he has to learn how to function in the normal world. The adolescent world is not the normal world, and this will set him or her up to fail.

Alternative peer group programs are the best possible place for a child who is returning from residential treatment. The parents should begin participating the moment they admit their child into residential treatment, so they are familiar with the program and have begun to make the changes needed to create a safe home for a teen in recovery.

Intensive Outpatient

Intensive outpatient treatment (IOP) provides at least ten hours per week of group therapy and is the most typical level of care for those being discharged from residential care. IOP is provided in both facilities and in private offices of licensed professionals. The client lives with his or her family and attends the group sessions three to four days per week. The insurance standard for discharge from intensive outpatient treatment is usually after ten weeks, although clients who remain in IOP much longer have fewer repeated episodes of treatment and three to four times the long-term success rates of those in shorter programs. The best programs keep clients in intensive outpatient for six to eight months, enough to actually change and stabilize habits.

Supportive Outpatient

Supportive outpatient treatment (SOP) is similar to the IOP level of care but requires less-frequent participation in group sessions. Most SOP clients attend group sessions several times per week for a period of around ten weeks.

Group Counseling

Group counseling is provided in some treatment facilities and in private practitioner offices to address issues associated with recovery. Often clients who have completed IOP and have become accustomed to live in sobriety will attend weekly group counseling sessions to help with secondary issues like dating, school, work, and family relationships.

Individual Counseling
Individual counseling or therapy is offered by licensed professionals in a variety of settings. Individual therapy is used to address problems that are unique to the individual and may be adjunctive to group counseling.

Family Counseling
Family counseling is helpful once all family members are capable of hearing feedback and accepting responsibility and have established clear boundaries. This will not work with family members who are incapable of looking at their own contribution to any dysfunction in the family. If the family is busy blaming each other and using their therapy time to report on the bad behavior of others, the family is not ready for family therapy.

Case Management
Case management is usually a function of one staff member in a residential, outpatient facility, or in an APG, whose responsibility it is to oversee and coordinate all aspects of a client's care.

Decisions
Consult others when making a treatment decision, and again before changing course once a plan has been initiated. Most teens in trouble have never finished anything they have started. They have never seen anything hard through to completion. Do not rob your teen of this experience even though you are hearing your child's very convincing argument that he or she is cured and the treatment center is just trying to milk you for money. I have heard this too often. Get to know the staff at the treatment facility. People who are interested in making a lot of money do not work there. A facility cannot keep a patient once that patient has met the criteria for discharge. Do not discharge your child until the professionals recommend it.

It is expensive. It is tempting to discount the treatment programs because it would be easier for you if you didn't have this bill to pay. You don't need a treatment facility that is built like a country club. Your teen doesn't need it. Your teen needs to develop some humility and gratitude. You need treatment professionals with some experience that you can trust. Most treatment professionals have years of experience with many teens, and you do not have that experience. Trust them.

When your child enters treatment, make the commitment to see it through to completion, to transition to a strong ongoing plan following the transition to lighter levels of care. Every transition from one level of care to another will introduce a little more freedom to your child. Freedom has not been safe for your child. His or her decisions without the safety of structure and support have not been good. Your family will be tested with each transition. You must be committed to stay the course. Finish what you start. This is not a short-term problem that can be fixed in a few months.

The adolescent's treatment professionals may recommend any of a variety of family activities including parental involvement in Al-Anon, sibling participation in Al-Ateen, or family participation in an alternative peer group program, if that is available. Involvement in treatment may mean that other people will know about the problem, your child may have to give up baseball or cheerleading, or your child's education may be interrupted in some way. Treatment for an adolescent means change for the whole family.

The whole family will need help dealing with this. Talk to friends and any local agency that provides alcohol and drug education for the community. They will be able to help you find a professional in the community who can guide you through this process. Families are units of interacting, moving pieces. Changes in one piece will create some changes in others.

When you choose a course of action, do not back out when it gets hard. It will get hard. I have seen parents move their child from one treatment program to another and then prematurely bring him home when he told them that the treatment was a waste of time and money, that it was a joke, that everyone was stupid, etc. I've seen parents do this and then sue the treatment facility for not managing the teen's treatment properly. It got hard. He didn't want to do it. Those families do not heal.

As you are working with a professional, consider the things that you are providing that make it possible for your child to self-destruct by using dangerous chemicals. If your child has access to cash, a car, or a cell phone, a drug deal is available at a moment's notice. They should be removed and earned back as trust is established. Remember, you cannot control your child's behavior. You can make it easy to keep drinking or using drugs or you can make it hard. At least do not contribute to making it easy.

Twelve-Step Communities

Twelve-step programs for adults have proliferated because they work. Many adults need treatment to get sober and the fellowship of a twelve-step recovery program to remain sober, and their spouse needs a codependent's twelve-step program for healthy functioning in the marriage. The same is true for adolescents and their families. The adult twelve-step community is not appropriate for adolescents, does not usually appeal to adolescents, and does not provide the oversight and accountability that teens require in consideration of their brain development. Further, twelve-step meetings for family members of adult substance abusers are often focused on spouses and are not easily adapted to parenting issues. Each person has to try a few different meetings and find the ones that really resonate.

I occasionally hear people say that twelve-step programs don't work. They do work. They are incredibly effective. However, they are not an inoculation that, once taken, heals you forever. If a person makes a tentative attempt and walks away after a brief exposure, there is nothing that will heal him or her until he or she is ready to commit. The twelve steps are a way of life that, if followed, will bring you incredible peace and serenity.

Alternative Peer Groups

The Alternative Peer Group (APG) provides a community of recovery for teens, parents, and often siblings (see www.aapg-recovery.com). The APG is exactly what the name indicates: a new peer group. The APG operates on the basis of positive peer pressure, strong accountability for healthy choices, and the fundamental importance of uniting the family. An APG consists of families with teens who are committed to recovery and a strong and talented staff who understand teens and parents and recovery. The parents work together in twelve-step fellowship, with sponsors and meetings. The teens work together in an environment of strict accountability in which the norms are honesty, integrity, and respect. The APG provides new peers for the adolescent, a new support system for the parents, and ideally a support system for the siblings. It creates the community that will establish and maintain recovery for the whole family.

The best APGs thrive because they are attractive to the kids. They make sobriety more fun than doing drugs, which says a lot. Most of the teens who begin this type of program say that they have never had so much fun. I work with an APG in Houston and have recently reviewed the outcomes of all of the kids who have completed our program since 2007 when I earnestly started keeping these kinds of records. To date, 95 percent of the adolescent graduates are productively engaged in a career, college, or graduate school. Seventy-one percent have maintained continued sobriety throughout the years. No other type of program can claim this level of success. The community works.

Finding an APG isn't so easy. One resource that is helpful is the Association of APGs in Houston, and another is the National Association of Recovery Schools.

School is usually the best place for kids to connect for drug distribution, so it's tough to stay in that environment and be sober if that's where your connections are. But moving to a new school will not help. Who are the easiest teens to become friends with in a new school? The druggies. They will hang out with anyone who will use drugs with them or has money. Find a recovery school (https://recoveryschools.org).

If your city or any city near you has an alternative peer group with a sober school, you have some great options. Insurance is not friendly to substance use, and most policies limit treatment to something that is so short that it is doomed to be ineffective. To stay in a healthy environment long enough to change habits means that you need a consistent group of peers who will support recovery and hold your teen accountable for wrong behavior for eighteen to thirty-six months. Parents and siblings need to participate in support and education in order for the family to recover.

It takes a very long time to turn this problem around. The research reported by Dr. Kitty Harris (1983) indicates that it takes as many months of treatment as the child spent using drugs in order to bring him to his normal level of functioning. Notice that I said "bring him" not "return him." You will not return to a previous point in time. Your child will mature through his development, commencing when his brain can begin to function normally. In an APG he will experience normal adolescence and be able to complete his treatment on solid ground.

References

Barry, C. L., McGinty, E. E., Pescosolido, B. A., Goldman, H. H. (2014) *Stigma, discrimination, treatment effectiveness, and policy: public views about drug addiction and mental illness.* Psychiatric Services. Oct;65(10):1269–72.

Blanton, B. *Radical Honesty: How to transform your life by telling the truth.* Stanley, VA: Sparrowhawk Publications, 1994.

Cates, J.C., Cummings, J. *Recovering Our Children*, New York: Writers Club Press, 2003.

Dahl, R. E. (2004) *Adolescent Brain Development: A period of vulnerability & opportunities.* Annals of NY Academy of Science, 1021:1–21 New York Academy of Sciences, p.8.

Fay, J. F., Billings, D. L. *From Innocence to Entitlement.* Golden, CO: Love and Logic Institute, 2005.

Giedd, J. N. (2015) "The Amazing Teen Brain." *Scientific American.* Jun;312(6):3–37.

Harris, K.S. *The developmental effects of alcoholism in the adolescent.* El Paso, TX: Substance Abuse Conference, Texas Tech University Health Sciences Center, 1983.

Hazelden (1998). *Day by Day: Daily Meditations for Recovering Addicts* (second edition). Center City, MI: Hazelden, 1998.

Meehan, B. *Beyond the Yellow Brick Road: Our children and drugs.* Kersey, CO: Meek Publishing Company, LLP, 1996.

Mendizza, M., Pearce, J.C. *Magical Parent Magical Child: The art of joyful parenting.* Berkeley, CA: North Atlantic Books, 2004.

Miniño, A.M. (2010). *Mortality among teenagers aged 12-19 years: United States, 1999–2006.* NCHS data brief, no 37. Hyattsville, MD: National Center for Health Statistics.

National Institute on Drug Abuse. *Understanding Drug Abuse and Addiction: What Science Says* Retrieved from http://www.drugabuse.gov/publications/teaching-packets/understanding-drug-abuse-addiction on August 9, 2015

Sannibale, C., Hurkett, P., van den Bossche, E., O'Connor, D., Zador, D., Capus, C., Gregory, K., McKenzie, M. (2003) *Aftercare attendance and post-treatment functioning of severely substance dependent residential treatment clients.* Drug Alcohol Rev. Jun;22(2):181–90.

Substance Abuse and Mental Health Services Administration. (2010). *Results from the 2009 National Survey on Drug Use and Health: Volume I. Summary of National Findings* (Office of Applied Studies, NSDUH Series H-38A, HHS Publication No. SMA 10-4586Findings). Rockville, MD.

Recommended Reading
for all Parents

Beattie, M. *Codependents Guide to the Twelve Steps*, New York: Simon & Schuster, 1990.

———. *The New Codependency: Help and Guidance for today's generation*. New York: Simon & Schuster, 2009.

Cates, J.C., Cummings, J. *Recovering Our Children*, New York: Writers Club Press, 2003.

Fay, J. F., Billings, D. L. *From Innocence to Entitlement*. Golden, CO: Love and Logic Institute, 2005.

Mandino, O. *The Greatest Miracle in the World*. New York: Bantam, 1977.

Meehan, B., Meyer, S. J. *Beyond the Yellow Brick Road*. Kersey, CO: Meek, 1996.

Ruiz, D. M. *The Four Agreements*. San Rafael, CA: Amber-Allen, 1997.

———. *The Mastery of Love: A practical guide to the art of relationships*. San Rafael, CA: Amber-Allen, 1999.

Smith, B., Wilson, B. *The Big Book of Alcoholics Anonymous*. San Bernardino, CA: Lark Publishing, LLC, 2013.

Barriers - lying

About the Author

Dr. Anette Edens left the world of finance to retrain as a psychologist when it became clear that her interests were more about people than investments. She joined the faculty of a small private university, where her research increasingly spotlighted the inadequacy of traditional treatment models to address the growing crisis of adolescent substance abuse. After the death of her youngest daughter, she dedicated herself to saving adolescent lives. This became her calling. She joined a group of passionate parents and advisors to develop and open a sober high school which has since grown into an exemplary model for recovery schools around the country. She opened a treatment program for young adults and their parents and began consulting with a young and brilliant counselor of like mind whose adolescent practice was perfect to introduce a parenting program to parallel the programming for the adolescents. By working with these families and using her own experiences with an alcoholic husband and troubled teen, she developed keen insight into the relationship between personal behavioral choices and the destructive behavior of others. Over more than twenty years she has provided innovative and effective approaches to emotional healing. Her work with families whose adolescents abuse substances has earned wide acceptance in the academic, professional, and recovery communities.

Made in the USA
Columbia, SC
16 May 2020